Soul Mates
and the
Zodiac

Soul Mates and the Zodiac

ATHENA STARWOMAN

Foreword by Deborah Gray

NH
NEW
HOLLAND

First published in Australia in 2005 by
New Holland Publishers (Australia) Pty Ltd
Sydney • Auckland • London • Cape Town

14 Aquatic Drive Frenchs Forest NSW 2086 Australia
218 Lake Road Northcote Auckland New Zealand
86 Edgware Road London W2 2EA United Kingdom
80 McKenzie Street Cape Town 8001 South Africa

10 9 8 7 6 5 4 3 2 1

National Library of Australia Cataloguing-in-Publication Data:

Starwoman, Athena.
        Soul mates and the zodiac.

        ISBN 1 74110 252 9.

        1. Astrology. 2. Love—Miscellanea. 3. Mate selection—
        Miscellanea. I. Title.

        133.5864677

Publisher: Fiona Schultz
Editor: Monica Berton
Designer: Joanne Buckley
Production Manager: Linda Bottari
Printer: McPherson's Printing Group, Victoria
Cover image: Getty Images
Back cover image: Athena Starwoman

Athena's Legacy Lives On

Athena Starwoman was and will always be, for eternity, my soul sister. She not only believed strongly in the power of dreams, but she lived every day as a magical awakening to her soul's true potential. What a great inspiration!

Athena innately believed that we are all adventurous souls who are reincarnated, and for as long as her fans and public wish it, Athena wanted her work and writings to continue to inspire well into the future. In fact, she was working on a number of worldwide projects throughout 2004 including books, columns and DVDs, right up to the time she passed on to her next life and next big adventure.

In 2004, during the weekend of the July full moon, Athena and I were wrapping up the filming of an in-depth interview with her for the 'Wish on a Spell' DVD, when Athena insisted that I ask her one more question. She wanted to discuss how she felt about the more sceptical elements of the media. 'Look, I've got a lot to thank the media and journalists for, after all, I've worked amongst them as a writer and colleague for many years,' she explained. 'But no matter how successful I've gone on to become, there will always be those who only want to ask me the same old boring questions like, "How much money have you made?" or "Is Athena Starwoman your real name?" What a waste of people's time! I often wonder why they don't ever sit down and really try to work out why it is that the public is so fascinated with the kind of work I, and others like me, do? Because let's face it, astrology and the study of the ancient mysteries have been going on for a very, very long time. It's been there since the beginning of philosophy, science and of course, astronomy. For as long as there are people on this and any other planet, there will always be huge public interest in all things magical and mystical. It's part of the never-ending human quest to understand the journey of the soul.

So why not get down to the nitty-gritty of it and ask me more valuable questions like, "How did you actually go about achieving your success?" or "What kind of philosophies in life have you followed to help you get there?" Give people some great techniques—wouldn't that be much more useful to their readers?'

To me, that's what Athena's work as a writer was really all about. Writing down as much as she could as she went about her travels, learning how to live and communicate better, not only to be more fulfilled within herself, but to divulge those hard-earned 'secrets' to as many people as she could. Even the most simple techniques of life are like a secret code to the uninitiated, and for Athena, writing her books and columns was the way she could give out all that valuable information to hundreds of thousands of people around the world. She wanted to share the techniques and wisdom she had gathered from a young age from not only great spiritual masters and magical teachers, but through her own personal revelations and constant epiphanies. Many times she'd excitedly share those personal revelations to me and others close to her; she was always so generous about that. She never cared about keeping the so-called 'secret formulas' to herself.

Recently one of Athena's friends remarked to me, 'You know it's really interesting that for such a relatively shy person who didn't really like big social gatherings at all, Athena sure got to be friends with an amazing and eclectic bunch of people.' And it's so true. From high-powered business brokers and jet-setting aristocrats, to nature-loving tree huggers and typical Aussie mums and dads, she got along with all of them. But she was always happiest socialising 'one on one'. And if she shone her magical light on you personally and shared her thoughts and time with you, it was an unforgettable and quite addictive experience (as well as a whole lot of Goddess-inspired fun).

In my opinion, that's the real key to the secret of her success as an author and columnist. It takes real talent and focus to be able to write the kind of words that speak 'one on one' to the reader. Yet, she always did just that, quite consciously and purposely. No matter what she was writing, she put her heart and soul into it. Of course, with her sassy grasp on pop culture and wickedly ironic sense of humour, she probably could've written a grocery list and made it interesting! Combining her talent for writing with her personal passion for astrology and spirituality, she couldn't possibly help but be so phenomenally successful in her chosen genre.

Athena speaks to you personally in her writing—she still does. In this book, and in the future through other projects she was working on, Athena wanted to continue to communicate one on one with her readers. She wanted to inspire your soul, uplift you with Goddess energy, enchant you with a sense of magic, give you hope and tickle your fanciful curiosity to go on and keep learning more and more and more. I've included some of our in-depth interview and personal chats below. One of the first questions I asked her was, 'What does astrology mean to you?'

'Astrology is tuning in to what's happening in the heavens in our solar system and observing the movement of the planets and stars and how they correspond and effect us here on earth. My view and techniques of astrology have greatly evolved since I first started studying astrology as a young girl. Astrology for me now is not so much about the exterior influences, but about the integration of the soul's journey. The soul's DNA can be read very well through the study of the stars and astrology, instead of it being a planetary energy with the separate planets, such as Venus (the Feminine-Goddess energy) or Mars (the Masculine-God energy) influencing us. I now see the planets and their different energies as actually being the different personas within us; the different levels of us that we have to integrate through different stages of our life as we journey into becoming One with the Sun, the Light, the Complete Being.

'I apply my knowledge of astrology daily, and it is a great tool. You can use it to help you make an important decision or to guide you to improving your relationships with others. But like any tool, you should also listen to your higher mind and your own inner voice because that will override anything—including an astrology reading if need be—because your inner voice is your greatest guide. For instance, the synchronicity of meeting my husband twelve years ago was an interesting example of how I chose to follow my inner voice, even though it conflicted with the planetary alignments and a whole range of other things that were going on in my life at the time.

'My father had just died and I was deeply affected by it. I became exhausted and just wanted to stay quietly inside my apartment in New York nurturing myself. But a friend of mine kept calling me and telling me to go to this Breakthrough Experience seminar presented by Dr John Demartini. But I really didn't want to go. I didn't feel like it. I just felt like being by myself for a while, and also Mercury was in retrograde, which is the planet of communication and travel, so this is usually not a good time to travel to another city and certainly not to go to a seminar about communication! So I kept resisting, saying no and avoiding it. The next night, right in the middle of a deep sleep, a strong voice woke me up and said, "Go to that seminar." But still I kept resisting. I kept making excuses not to go and I even threw some coins "betting" on heads I go and tails I don't. Three times I threw the coins and three times it landed heads. And the strong voice in my mind kept waking me up in the middle of the night saying, "Go to that seminar." So even though Mercury was in retrograde, and I had not felt like going, I *had* to listen to that voice. I knew enough from my life's experiences not to ignore my higher voice, especially when it was calling so strongly. So, I finally went and had a fantastic time at the seminar, learning about The Demartini Method (the Collapse Process). I also met my soul mate, my husband, Dr John Demartini, who is also a great spiritual and inspirational guide in my life.'

How does magic fit in with astrology?

'Living with a sense of magic is an integral part of what I do and feel on a daily basis. The art of magic can use elements of the more established forms of astrology, as well as the more esoteric. Magic can also be tuning in way beyond our own solar system to the cosmic systems far beyond that and looking into the mysteries of life—which incorporates more than what is going on in just our universe. Because there are many universes, we can learn to tune into them as well. By using the "super space" inside ourselves, the intuitive side of ourselves can connect us to the "super universe" and connect us to things that we don't even see or know about on earth yet.

'I always say that if you don't believe in magic, then how can magic believe in you? If you don't believe in yourself, why would other people believe in you? I think it's really important for everyone to know about the mystical side of themselves. Don't miss out on those things because life is so full of enchanted and miraculous moments—you just have to take the time to look around and notice them. For instance, on your birthday people might say to you, "Make a wish and it will come true." Well I say, don't just wait for your birthday to make a wish. Why not do it every day? Because, after all, every day is a brand new day of your life with new opportunities and new challenges. Once you start doing this, and being aware of your eternal soul, it can absolutely change your life.'

So how did you get the name Starwoman?

'The name Starwoman came into my life quite naturally and I believe that it chose me. An American Indian, a shaman, called me by that name. I met him when I was studying astrology at the Eselan Institute in California in the early 1970s. When I was introduced to him he immediately started calling me "Starwoman". He went on to "christen" me with that name in a magical ceremony. That was a very strong experience for me and really changed my life. It was even more profound for me because that American Indian ceremony, the "name-giving" if you like, was also my very first christening. I was never christened in a church because my father thought it was better for me to wait until I was old enough to choose my own religion. It was like he had some kind of predictive sense of what was awaiting me. So when the shaman took me through that wonderfully magical ceremony and dipped a big feather into the ocean foam and wet my hair with it and named me "Starwoman", that really meant everything, because it was my first "naming ceremony" of any kind. "Starwoman" became part of me completely; it is who I am in every way. It's how I live my life, spiritually, mentally and philosophically.

'The shaman's name was Don Jose, from the Huichol tribe in Nayarit, Mexico. One of the professors at the college had studied with him and brought Don Jose from his village in Mexico to California. Don Jose was a tiny man and nuggety, but when you were in his presence, a part of you felt totally humbled. He'd make quick movements like a bird. He had skin like a coconut shell and beady black eyes that looked right through you, but whatever truly magical people have, well, he had it—that shaman presence.

'Having the name Starwoman has been both a pain and a pleasure, because when I came back to Australia in the 1970s, a few people probably thought I'd gone out of my mind! But let's face it, I am in a field that is 'out of this world', so I couldn't have been called something like Athena Smith because it probably wouldn't have resonated the right energy. All names, magic or otherwise, definitely vibrate their energies around you. Sometimes, if I ever feel a bit rundown or tired, I may choose to call myself "Earth Woman" to ground myself, but it doesn't last long because I prefer flying off among the planets. I feel right at home there!'

Athena wanted her writings to continue not only as her legacy, but to remind her readers and fans that no matter what you've experienced in life, soul mates can be found and dreams really can come true. Luckily for us (as the writings of Nostradamus will attest), the very nature of astrology, its predictions and spirituality, can be written years, if not millennia, ahead.

Deborah Gray

Contents

Introduction

This book is a star guide to finding your other half, twin self or soul mate. It is also a guide to opening your heart and learning to love from a totally new universal level. The principles of astrology and a general understanding of the zodiac can help you recognise the soul mate of your dreams. It is said that once you learn the make-up of each sign, you can have a true understanding of each vibrational level of the zodiac.

Experiencing true love on a deep, spiritual level isn't easy; some people spend their entire lives searching for the one person who makes them feel complete. Finding your soul mate or twin self is the pinnacle of your earthly existence, so never, ever give up—no matter how many times you fall in and out of love.

May you discover your soul mate and may your sacred soul mate journey be one of love.

The Soul Mate Connection

The greatest quest on earth is to find your own true star mate.

When you are tuned in to your soul and understand the 'real you', the possibility of meeting your soul mate is heightened. When you aren't tuned in to your soul or following the messages of your heart, even if you were to meet your soul mate, you probably wouldn't know it because you are not complete in the cycle of love evolution. The cycle of love evolution is the process of 'learning to love'. Throughout your life you encounter many different love experiences—each one bringing you closer to a complete understanding of yourself, and ultimately, recognition of your soul mate through that understanding. If you haven't reached a point where you understand yourself, your soul mate could be standing right in front of you and you would look in the other direction for a partner!

People often refer to soul mates in the same league as relationships in general. This 'soul mate' term is commonly interpreted as a variety of experiences from close friendships, family connections and past or present romantic attachments to long-time marriage partnerships. But you can have all kinds of spiritual connections with other people or beings, including friends, relatives and even pets you have shared time and space with in other lifetimes. These connections help you to learn and grow, preparing you for the final stage of love evolution when you meet and recognise your true soul mate. Each spiritual connection is simply a prelude to your ultimate destination—the reunification of your soul halves. And though many of our most meaningful relationships in this lifetime would fall into this soul-connection category, the true meaning of the term 'soul mate' is something very unique and far beyond the realm of most of your every day relationship exchanges. It resonates on an entirely different level because your soul mate is the other long-separated part of you—your perfect other half that merges to complete your soul.

According to mysticism, it is said that when a complete soul comes to earth to begin its physical learning experience, before it reaches the dense levels of our atmosphere, the soul's essence divides into two individual people. It does this so that the separate halves can complete their cycle of worldly experience and evolve into a more complete, loving being. These two separated individuals (the soul mates) represent the physical earthly embodiment of the male and female halves of the one soul. Therefore, a soul mate represents only one special person—*the unique other half of yourself or the perfectly matched other half of your soul that completes you*—and no other relationship, no matter how special it may be, can do this. Your soul mate makes you 'whole' again when the essence of your souls reconnect.

But dealing with a soul mate is generally not a simple or easy-flowing process; it often involves pain, sacrifice and, sometimes, disillusionment. Because we often sense in our hearts and souls the kind of partner we are looking for, it can come as quite a shock to find that being with a soul mate could be more than we bargained for! Sometimes your soul mate may fall short of your expectations or even be tough to understand or live with. Just because someone is your true other half doesn't mean that you are walking into a happily-ever-after relationship. In fact, often the opposite applies, and you may find that both you and your true other half have lessons to learn in this lifetime, either together or separately. When this is the case, there are often emotionally intense growing pains ahead.

Connecting with your soul mate can be extremely unsettling and disturbing. Because your soul mate is so psychically and emotionally attuned to you and can make you happier than anyone else can, they also have the ability to break your heart and make you extremely sensitive as well. And meeting a true soul mate is no assurance that you are destined to stay together. You may have many meetings over many lifetimes before you are both evolved enough to be able to reconnect on all levels of existence again and return to a oneness of being in all areas of your mind, body and soul.

Being with your soul mate can open up a whole new range of conscious and unconscious emotional responses with anxiety, uncertainty and fear being part of these feelings. Why? Because instinctively and unconsciously, a soul mate knows how to push all your emotional buttons and can cause the ultimate extremes of pleasure and pain! To expect a soul mate relationship to flow trouble-free is unrealistic. If any relationship can lift you to the dizzying heights of heaven or drag you down to the depths of hell, a soul mate connection can. No wonder so many people actually run away from soul mate relationships rather than towards them, particularly men who become frightened by the depth of the relationship experience! The intensity of the unconscious feelings that can be evoked can be overwhelming and make some people feel vulnerable beyond their levels of emotional endurance.

Even so, eventually in one lifetime, if not this one, you are destined to come face-to-face with your true other half and deal with the consequences of this meeting. And when you do, if you are prepared to go the 'emotion churning' distance and look upon this relationship as the most meaningful and fulfilling of life's experiences, you'll discover that the soul mate connection is the ultimate emotional flowering. It's a chance to evolve from two separate individuals into one soul again. It is the subliminal quest that we are all embarking on because reuniting with your true half represents becoming whole again. It completes your journey to your ultimate destination and evolution—the union of your soul halves.

Like the greatest love affairs—from Romeo and Juliet, Tristan and Isolde to Cleopatra and Mark Antony—your personal journey through life is a mission of love, because what drives you knowingly or unconsciously is your constant unrelenting search for your soul mate and your destiny to reconnect with them again. Forces far beyond our comprehension control our lives and, although we may not realise it, we are always on a quest to meet our soul mate. That's why so many of us feel our life is nothing but a heart-wrenching soap opera at times.

Words like 'romance', 'love' and 'passion' are bandied around and greatly commercialised in movies, on television and in romantic novels. But our soul mate quest is a love story with a difference—it is a journey for a love that surpasses all others. A soul love is so different from a casual romantic fling that it is like comparing the mighty ocean to a drop of water. Where an earthly casual passion is a short-term experience or adventure, a soul mate relationship expands its boundaries to far beyond infinity until, eventually, soul mate reunites with soul mate. It is everybody's true love story. It is a story about life, rebirth, reincarnation and beyond. It is the story of the ethereal heart of our spiritual soul completing itself.

Your Soul Mate Story

Have you met your soul mate? Lots of people believe they have already met their soul mate in some form or fashion. Many people use the term 'soul mate' to describe a partner, a best friend, a teacher or guru, and even a lover they are connected with, who is the same sex as themselves. I've even heard some people claim they feel a special soul mate connection with a pet (I once had a dog named Max that seemed to be able to tune into my very soul and I into his, so I know what they mean when they make this claim). Therefore, it is no wonder that most of us think that a 'soul mate' is someone or something that we come into contact with or relate to in a predestined or magical or mystical way.

In everyday terms, our soul mate connections are hinted at and sometimes even dreamt about, but frequently they are totally misunderstood. Often your true soul mate connection is not the same as the physical chemistry you feel for a work colleague. It is not the 'crush' in your teen years or those déjà vu experiences you sometimes have with others that make you feel as if you saw a flash of a past lifetime together. It's not even those connections you feel for places, pets, pieces of antique jewellery, houses or other such items.

While you may think that you've met your soul mate, it is most likely that they are a soul friend or sometimes even a soul enemy. I mention soul enemies because we all experience positive energy flows and negative energy exchanges with people in our lifetime. Positive exchanges can draw us to a person, while negative exchanges can repulse us. By nature there are some people we like and others that we don't. These chemical responses can build up, expand and become stronger, as if fate is propelling us towards that other person, lifetime after lifetime.

As an example, have you ever met a person that everyone around you is raving about, saying how wonderful they are? But when you meet this person, they make your skin crawl and you can't explain this innermost sense to anyone, but you also can't deny it. Instinctively—even intuitively—you don't connect with this person. It may be that this individual is someone you have battled with in a previous life and in this lifetime your deep-seated soul memory recognises them from the past and remembers how they caused you grief. Your soul memory automatically and unconsciously repels you away from this person.

It is important to realise that many people tend to consider a number of individuals they meet under fateful conditions as their soul mates. And as stated earlier, while it is possible to have deep and meaningful spiritual connections between yourself and other individuals (or a pet), a soul mate connection can only be forged with your perfect other half.

A true soul mate, as the name implies, is not just a special relationship you can have with many close associates; it is the true mate or complimentary half of your own unique soul. There is only one real perfect half or soul mate for you. According to ancient studies of the Bible and other books like the *Egyptian Book of the Dead* and the *Tibetan Book of the Dead*, the meaning of 'soul mate' is the one individual who at the soul levels of operation completes you.

Why Do People Seek Their Soul Mate?

Most of us acknowledge that there are many levels of existence in both the seen or known world and the unseen or unknown world. We come into this earth world when we are born and we depart it when we die. Every night when we go to sleep, we disappear from the everyday world and enter into the sleep or dream world. Therefore, if we claim that no 'other worlds' exist—apart from the everyday existence on the earth world that we live in—this would mean that we were born out of nothing and go back to nothing. Anyone who has studied physics knows that this statement is not correct. Everything has to come from something because according to the law of conservation of energy, energy is never lost, it is simply transformed from one form to another. Everything comes from something and goes back to something. As a very easy example, look at water as it evolves through its earthly cycle. Water falls from the sky in the form of rain. It gets heated by the sun and turns into steam. It then returns back to the sky and comes back down again as rain. Water can be an ice cube, it can be vapour or steam, and it can be so solid that you can't break it. It can take many forms and so can our expression of life too. We have lived at one time as a seed being fertilised by sperm in the womb (visible only through a special microscope). We have lived as a baby, a child, an adolescent, or a totally grown individual.

It is said in many of the great ancient teachings of wisdom that when a complete soul (which is termed the 'soul seed') enters the denser realms of the earth (the magnetosphere, which is the dense magnetic field that surrounds the earth), that's when it separates into two individual and incomplete halves (called the soul mates). These two separated parts are the male and female side of you. That way when you enter the world, your soul, through its twin halves, can have every form of experience as both a male and female, and learn how to be a creator on the next levels of the cosmic chain of creation. Once reunited, your twin halves complete a total realm of earthly experience capable of understanding higher spiritual love.

The moment you separate from your perfect half at the earth's outer levels of density, you then begin your sacred soul journey on earth in two separated forms—the male and female—but your connection on the most subtle spiritual subliminal levels is never severed or broken. You are always in psychic or cosmic-connected communication with your other half. That's why so many people dream about their soul mates, rather than meet them on the everyday levels of operation.

So, although in our physical everyday world we may feel separated from our soul mate, in true cosmic and infinite terms, there is no real separation. This sense of separation exists only within the physical levels of knowledge and operation. You cannot really be separated from your soul mate on the higher spirit or spiritual heart levels, because your soul mate is *you* in another body or physical form. You are only separated by earthly distance, density and ignorance—not by any higher spiritual boundaries. If you can tap into those higher spiritual levels through meditation, dreams or by opening your heart with gratitude, you can feel a strong connection to your soul mate and may even be able to communicate with them through thought powers, or catch a vision of their face in your mind's eye.

Remember, your soul mate is a part of *you* in another body of the opposite sex. That's why many of us know this innately and miss our soul mates terribly. Even in everyday busyness, for those who are highly attuned and cosmically aware of their soul mate's existence, it is the soul or spiritual part of yourself that is intuitively sensed as 'missing'. That's why many people often dream about their soul mates and reconnect with them on higher ethereal levels, and not so often on the more limited physical levels of everyday operation.

People seek their soul mate because this individual is the only other perfect person who can complete their existence and fulfil their soul's desires. They, and only they, have the special spiritual essence of *you* within them, and this is the higher power that can and will eventually return you to one soul again. Your soul mate brings you back to the higher soul levels of operation, when you truly join your spiritual hearts.

According to ancient mystical teachings, in reality, very few people actually unite with their real soul mate. They may cross paths with them and even spend time with them, but to make a higher spiritual connection takes a tremendous amount of love, dedication and compassion. Not many people in the everyday modern world have the kind of awareness or tolerance needed to make that connection. In addition, to truly connect with your soul mate, both soul halves need to be operating on high levels of spiritual consciousness and self-awareness, otherwise you will not recognise each other. It is only through the understanding and acceptance of unconditional love that you are able to connect with your soul mate. Unconditional love is learned and experienced through your spiritual connections with others, by being grateful for your earthly experiences (both good and bad), by opening up your heart, and letting go of illusive judgments.

In life, most of us don't really have much of an idea about who we really are in terms of our true soul self. Some of us are so busy just surviving and getting by that we don't have a chance to really look into our own heart and soul to find out what is shining within our own essence of being. We can spend most of our lives hiding behind social masks, facades, business professionalism, and the identity we present to the world when we 'pretend' to be someone we are not. The first step to meeting your soul mate is to awaken and discover your true individual soul identity—the real you. By adopting a universal perspective (seeing the big picture), and accepting that there are no wrong, right, good or bad experiences in life, you overcome the need for false or preconceived responses, thus freeing your true personality. To really connect with your soul mate you need to have an awakened, centred and balanced one-level personality, not many different levels of personality. It is your splintered personas or imbalanced perceptions of yourself that will attract you to relationships with individuals who help you to justify these split identities. In relationships, sometimes we aren't looking for the truth, but for someone who can justify in the outer world our own inability to live our heart and soul's higher purpose.

So will you recognise your soul mate when you meet them? The answer to this question is both 'yes' and 'no'. Sometimes people feel something powerful has hit them when they first meet their soul mate, and other times they don't feel a thing. So your initial response to meeting someone is no guarantee that you will even sense you are soul mates (if, indeed, you are fortunate enough to meet each other in this lifetime). For example, you may sit next to each other on an airplane, grow up in the same neighbourhood, or be friends at college, but so many pieces of the cosmic jigsaw have to fall into place accurately for the real soul mate connection to be recognised. The circumstances may not be right for you to develop the relationship at the time you meet, or your age differences or sense of 'self-knowledge' about your true identity may not be at a stage where spending time together in a relationship would be successful or even a possibility. You may not be interested in each other romantically. You may not be wise enough to know what true love is or what your soul mate would be like until you become more and more aware within yourself. At various stages of your own soul and identity development, you will be attracted to individuals who fit your personality at that level of your development. And if your soul mate isn't resonating on exactly the same development level as you are, you could be living on different vibrational fields of experience. They may be going north, while you are going south, or, they may be only interested in blondes, while you are a brunette. Your false beliefs or preferences could deter your actual progress in meeting your soul mate. Until you are truly awakened spiritually or understand your 'earth-sensed values', which create your personal tastes, goals and forge your romantic desires, you will not recognise your true soul's identity (if it were totally formed and free to choose for you). That's why so many people go 'looking for love in all the wrong places', as they say. It's also why we use the term 'lost soul'. With no connection or link with your own personal soul, you are likely to be disconnected from your soul mate forever, because you will not recognise each other.

When it comes to soul-connecting with your true other half, extraordinary circumstances or feelings often dictate your meeting and recognition. Meeting your soul mate is something you will long remember, like the frozen frames of a movie that is somehow implanted and replayed over and over again in the memory banks of your soul. There is an inner sense of wholeness or completion when you finally reconnect with your soul mate, and a certainty that you belong together. It's one thing to meet your soul mate, but another thing to connect with them. A soul mate connection needs to occur under the right conditions. To make this bond grow and to merge your lives together and become 'one', you both need to be open-hearted and fully aware of your soul in order to get to know each other on equal terms. You not only have to connect on the soul levels, you also have to make this relationship work on the everyday levels of existence. And that is a super-challenge!

So remember that, even if you are fortunate enough to meet your soul mate and actually find yourself spending time with them or dating them, the success of the relationship depends on how attuned you are to yourself, which determines whether or not you can connect with them. If you don't really 'know' yourself, you are not likely to recognise your own other half. You have to find yourself to find them. In fact, I believe that two soul mates often meet each other, and may even become close, but they don't stay together in a lasting relationship because one, or both of them, is not personally evolved enough to really appreciate that they have found their soul mate. It's important to realise that, at most times, this reconnection of the two separated souls is so powerful and deep that it is actually more difficult to be in a soul mate relationship than a transient, less heart-connected one. A soul-connected relationship impacts the individual on so many unconscious levels that it can be exhausting and quite testing in many ways.

Dates of the Zodiac

- Aries   21 March–20 April
- Taurus   21 April–21 May
- Gemini   22 May–21 June
- Cancer   22 June–22 July
- Leo   23 July–23 August
- Virgo   24 August–22 September
- Libra   23 September–23 October
- Scorpio   24 October–22 November
- Sagittarius 23 November–21 December
- Capricorn   22 December–20 January
- Aquarius   21 January–18 February
- Pisces   19 February–20 March

These dates should be used as a guide only. If you were born at the beginning or end of a sign (sometimes called the 'cusp'), it's a good idea to have a natal (birth) chart prepared, which uses your time, date and place of birth to determine the position of the Sun at the exact moment you were born.

The Zodiac and your Soul Mate

The principles of astrology and a general understanding of the zodiac can help you recognise the soul mate of your dreams. The signs of the zodiac play a big role in our earthly incarnations and evolution. It is said that we live many different lifetimes, born under each sign of the zodiac—starting with Aries and ending with Pisces. Once we learn the values, lessons and principles of one sign, we are then ready to be reborn into the next and so on, until we have experienced life under the influence of each sign. Eventually, through this process, we gain a full understanding of each vibrational level of the zodiac—and ultimately, of ourselves.

The compatible and incompatible energy that exists between two people defines the success or failure of that relationship. But how do you know if you and your lover are well matched? Astrology has always offered remarkable insight into the chemistry that exists between two people. By understanding the signs of the zodiac and the fundamental energy vibration that each one represents, unlocking the mysteries of the soul mate connection becomes a little easier.

The following astrological guide will help you recognise your soul mate. It provides examples to consider when meeting someone of each sign of the zodiac who you think may be your potential soul mate.

Star Guys
Mr Aries Soul Mate

Be warned...some Aries men can have a long list of women they have experienced intense magical and physical/sexual connections with. This trait can lead them to temporarily misread or misinterpret a connection as soul bonding (particularly under the intoxicated physical spell of strong chemistry like sexual attraction and magnetism).

If an Aries man is your soul mate you can expect amazing sparks to fly—but be warned, these can happen on both positive and negative levels because there will be lots of energy being played out between you and it may be hard to channel it wisely. Even at the very beginning, this soul mate connection often starts with a flash of lightning, with a romantic movie-like meeting, which can leave your head spinning. Whether it happens at the time of meeting or not, sooner or later, you are likely to experience strong chemistry if this Aries man is truly your soul mate. In fact, the earth could seem to move, tremble or even noticeably rock beneath your feet! When the initial shock of meeting your Aries man is over (which could take several weeks, months or years), to test that he is your true soul mate and not simply a very attractive heart-stopping infatuation, you need to put him on the cosmic soul spot. When you are both together in a relaxed situation (not in a crowded shopping centre or somewhere with lots of action or distractions), get your potential Aries soul mate's attention. Once you can sense that he is totally focused on you (not watching the sports on television or looking at his watch out of the corner of his eyes), open up your heart and project your inner feelings to him, preferably without the use of words. To achieve this open-hearted state you need to put yourself in a mental place where you can focus on how much gratitude and thankfulness you have within you because you have met this man. This will forge a very strong heart-connection between you both, particularly if he feels the same way about you. As mentioned earlier, feelings can speak far more loudly than words, and you should be able to get your Aries man to tune in to you and achieve a heart-to-heart connection with or without dialogue. If you feel you need to speak your 'thank-fulness' and the blessings of being in this relationship out loud, trust your inner intuition in this situation.

Whether words are used or not, this cosmic connection between you is likely to be more subtle on an unconscious-ness level of togetherness rather than through a casual chat or conversation. It is designed to take place and open up the higher psychic soul levels of communication and operation, rather than on the more earthbound physical realms of the physical or bodily senses. It is up to you to use the right ingredients, thoughts or words to create an open-hearted loving state of psychic and spiritual exchange that is often experienced between two soul mates, because this connec-tion simply needs to capture the truth that there is a oneness between you and this person.

To create the right mood or circumstances may take some planning on your part. You may need to organise a situation where you are together listening to music, dancing, sharing laughter, or just being in a quiet place and sharing an experience such as watching the sun rise or set. You could even be making love. When you feel you have created this higher soul-connection between you, and you 'know' within yourself that your heart is really open with love for this man, now is the time to put your soul test to work. Once you have all these things in place, look deeply and meaningfully into his eyes. If he isn't your true soul mate he probably won't be able to comfortably hold your gaze for very long—he can only do this when he has a real soul mate connection with you. If he's uncomfortable making eye contact, then he's probably not 'the one' or you have not opened your heart to a state of thankfulness and he may be sensing some of your insecurities, rather than the higher soul love that you want to give to him. If he holds your gaze and returns it with equal intensity, then there is a strong likelihood that he has a true heart love and (possibly even soul) connection with you.

This test is just a beginning and a great way to explore the soul mate possibility between you. However, magic moments between non-soul mate relationships occur very frequently so you need to look for more obvious cosmic connections between you as well. You need to sense his soul and observe how he responds to exploring his higher connections with you.

Now there are usually clues to help you check this soul mate connection out. Some possible examples are when he suddenly phones you when you are thinking of him, almost as though he has read your thoughts, or if he buys you a gift that you have wanted him to give you or dreamed about him giving you. Unusual coincidences need to occur between you too.

Obviously there are many ways to see if he can sense or feel you; you can probably come up with your own special way of doing this. What you are looking for is whether he can unconsciously tune into your needs and hidden desires because, if he is your soul mate, somehow he'll be able to fulfil some of your most deep-seated desires or dreams as if by magic. In addition, other cosmic connections are likely to occur. He may say the same thing as you at exactly the same time or go to hold your hand at the exact same moment you reach for his. In real soul mate connections, there are times when your everyday and unconscious thought patterns overlap and become 'one' and that is what you are looking to observe in Mr Aries.

When it hits home and the potential erupts that perhaps there is more to this relationship that just an infatuation or fanciful attraction, an Aries man falls hard, particularly when he really makes a soul mate connection. But be aware that some Aries men can have a long list of women they have experienced intense magical and physical/sexual connections with and this can lead them to temporarily misread or misinterpret your connection as soul bonding (particularly under the intoxicated physical spell of strong chemistry like sexual attraction and magnetism).

But maturity is often a great teacher of wisdom for Mr Aries, particularly when he is older. When an Aries man really connects, he usually knows it subliminally, even if at the time this connection occurs, he doesn't appreciate or even consider the true 'soul mate' significance of his feelings. He may just think he has met a very special person. But whether he recognises the connection or not, once his soul is connected, the Aries man can become dramatically bewitched, besotted and enchanted with his soul mate. If he is insecure and feels threatened by his emotions, or he believes his attentions are not being returned in the same way, he may even become obsessive or irrational. Sometimes his feelings can frighten him, particularly when he is overwhelmed by the unusual depth and significance of what he is sensing, and in some cases this feeling can make an Aries run for cover.

Also remember that beneath his somewhat cool, flippant demeanour, an Aries man is often masking extreme insecurities, even though he would be the last person to admit it and is often in denial of them.

If you think an Aries man is your soul mate, remember that Aries is a fire sign, which means he is intensely passionate and overdramatic at times. So, even in a soul-mate relationship, he's either going to be hot on your trail or cold as ice. Because of this, your relationship with him could still be a testing one. Any arguments or compromises you may need to make in order to keep life harmonious may need to be on his terms as he treads warily and gingerly along the soul mate journey. This is part of the total 'connection' and growing soul experience you will share with him. You are likely to be his right arm, his inspiration, his guiding or leading light, even though he won't admit this to you (except possibly in very private moments).

While the Aries man has a volatile side that can erupt anywhere and at any time, his truest love feelings operate so deep within him that it is often not apparent, even to him. So while your Aries man may have an occasional fiery emotional outburst, and sometimes lack the ability to express his sincerest love and regard for you, the bonus is that he is one of the zodiac's most romantic, ardent, stimulating and exciting soul mate heroes. When you have an Aries man as your possible soul mate, you are embarking upon a sometimes stormy, highly passionate, testing and frequently traumatic love journey of a lifetime, so shield yourself in advance and be prepared for moments of doubt.

His Virtues
The Aries man is sexy, attractive and offers stimulating company and loads of fun. He will help you learn new things and keep you growing—particularly regarding the real meaning of unconditional soul love. He has the power to keep you young at heart and he is seldom boring.

His Vanities
The Aries man can be the 'little boy' who never grew up (something of a Peter Pan character). He can burn out your patience and not know when enough is enough. He can be extremely selfish and demanding and sometimes even irritatingly immature. He can be irrational and overly dramatic. He can exaggerate the smallest trivial thing and blow it out of

proportion. He is also afraid of being emotionally vulnerable and this can make him run away from a strong soul encounter rather than value it for the true blessing that has found him.

Mr Taurus Soul Mate

If you discover your soul mate is a Taurus man, expect Cupid's love arrow to hit hard. Wild horses couldn't drag you apart and you may spend most of your time entangled in each other's embrace.

A Taurus man is a tough guy to work out. He is a deep thinker and tends to hold back when it comes to expressing his feelings or his excitement. Usually the realisation that this relationship could be a soul-connected one will either start with high passion and amazing chemistry that sizzles on a very noticeable level, or the connection sneaks up on you slowly and quietly and comes as a surprise one day (or night) in the future. If the relationship starts with high passion, naturally you'll know immediately. The chemistry and sexual desire between you will hit every cell and molecule and you'll tingle all over. Wild horses couldn't drag you apart and you may spend most of your time entangled in each other's embrace.

Passion is important for Taurus people, even if they don't reveal this need to others. After all, Taurus is ruled by Venus, the sensual, touchy-feely planet, so when the love bug hits, it is a powerful force. Keep in mind that Venus's passion does not necessarily mean a soul mate connection, so even a highly charged, passionate beginning to a relationship does not always guarantee you've met your perfect half—you'll have to watch for many other signs as well. In many cases, the Taurus male (who takes every step in life with caution), doesn't always allow his high passion to erupt immediately. Like an underground volcano, his desire ignites in a hidden and often slow-boiling fashion, which takes its own special magical time to reveal its true force (and soul mate significance). That's why it can take some time to suddenly realise you've been bewitched by Mr Taurus!

In extreme cases, it is very possible that you'll be friends with Mr Taurus for quite some time before you even consider that you may have a soul mate connection. The Taurus man lives in a private world and has many hidden depths of feeling within him, and the space between you both can be so distant at times, that in the beginning you might even fix him up with one of your girlfriends. However, time might suddenly reveal to you just how much you want him for yourself, and then you'll discover you are anxious to alter the energy exchange between you from friendship to love, and to move on to an even higher soul mate connection. So be wary of burning any romantic bridges behind you when you are dealing with a Taurus man, because if you aren't careful, you may have to do some smart manoeuvring to win him back.

But relationships with any Taurus man are never really as straightforward as they seem. Why a Taurus man can be so contradictory or difficult to fathom is because he is often not really in touch with his own feelings. He can close down his heart, rather than open it. Because he lives so much in the material and physical realms rather than in the emotional or psychic realms, the subtle call of true or soul love might have to give him a strong rap on his heartstrings (more so than other signs) for him to get the cosmic love message. Even then he won't jump to immediate conclusions about the depth and potential of this relationship, even if he does merrily (and sometimes hastily) jump into bed.

What Mr Taurus does or says—and what he deeply 'feels'—are often two dramatically different things. His physical side of expression greatly differs from his emotional side. In other words, he may be your greatest experience of a lover, but that doesn't necessarily go hand-in-hand with him loving you. He may jump merrily into bed with someone he doesn't have strong feelings for, but he will take his time going into a sexual relationship with someone he has deep feelings for. By this statement, I don't mean that he won't hastily jump into bed with someone he cares for, just that he can be cautious around people who can penetrate his emotional reserve. Because of his natural level of sensual and sexual operation, Mr Taurus is an individual who can make love without being emotionally connected to the person he is making love to. In fact, the two areas can often be quite far apart in his inner-most core of feeling.

Usually when a Taurus man makes a real heart and soul connection, he moves very slowly towards commitment because he likes to keep the magical moments of his life, or his secret inner-felt 'treasures', forever. He's a practical thinker and yet he's also naturally cautious. But he also hates to make mistakes and to have to live with them. He'd rather settle for your friendship and the long-term values that can be forged between you, than risk losing you through a failed cloud nine romance that hits the high chords of desire, but has no real staying power. He likes grounded commitment. Being practical in nature he craves commitment, but is also deeply afraid of making one. Sometimes he has to be forced to commit, especially if he is quite content to settle into a long-term courtship, rather than a long-term relationship! But if you show him you're his for keeps and win his trust, he'll spoil you with romance and passion.

However, soul mate or not, keep in mind that the Taurus man feels more in control when he doesn't rush into things. He likes to take plenty of time making any big commitment, so don't back him into a tight corner unless you've been waiting for many years! Also, try to get along well with his old girlfriends, mother or sisters because, even if he acts like he's not really close to them, because of his ruler Venus, all the women in his life are very important to him. Women represent his attachment to Venus and should not be treated disrespectfully.

So how do you discover whether you have a soul mate connection with Mr Taurus? Talk about the future in vague open-ended ways and then ask him what he wants his life to be like in, say, three years time. If he feels a bond with you, he'll include you in his answer (or a place for someone special in his life if he doesn't want to be so specific about mentioning you in particular). In some cases, his plans will be wonderfully inclusive of you. If he gives you a vague 'I don't know' answer and doesn't want to share his future thoughts with you, you may have to resort to Plan B. Give him a big, warm hug and hold on (physical action often works best with a Taurus man, rather than asking him to think about things). If you have a soul mate connection, he'll get lost in the moment and hug you back in the same way. If he pushes you back, starts to pat you on the back, or politely pulls away, and then noticeably changes the subject, you may have to be patient and try again at a later date. There is the likelihood that he isn't your soul mate, but that isn't black or white yet.

What's important is that you don't push too hard. Testing him can take a long time because prior to making any kind of true commitment, he's generally a slow mover and easily pulls up the drawbridge to his heart if he feels someone is attempting to trespass on his holiest of sacred ground—his soul space.

If your Taurus man fails dismally in one of your soul mate tests, or there are times when he is distant and he puts up his emotional or communication guard, heed this word of warning: Don't be too hasty to write him off as a soul mate. Remember that Mr Taurus is an earth sign, so don't misinterpret his extremely cautious ways to mean disinterest. He often takes his time to show his true soul colours. He can be tough when it comes to certain emotional or soul issues. If you do have a special soul bond with him and as an individual you're a bit pushy, independent, a tomboy, a successful businessperson or a trendsetter, you could be a major challenge to him. You will have some head-butting in your future together, because he likes to be in charge (just like the bull that he is). Therefore, it is in your best interests to be super-feminine and a bit dependent on him. If you're really clever and good at what you do, that could be one more reason why, at times, he may be distant. Amazingly, even the most modern Taurus man can still be a bit old-fashioned about what a 'woman' should be like (even if you couldn't guess it from being around him). But if the soul bond between you is true and strong, whether you are Miss Feminine or Ms Feminist, you won't let petty earthly stuff close down the communication links between you, unless you close down your hearts to each other.

To ensure your soul mate journey together is one of higher love, do whatever you can (practice patience, tolerance, compassion and understanding) to give each other a chance to learn more and more about love. Do whatever you can to keep your hearts open. In hard times, sit down and write all the benefits you offer each other and read them until your hearts open up to each other again. As you are dealing with a Taurus you need to watch that you don't begin to test each other by becoming stubborn or judgmental. If you can refrain from competing with one other (to see who can control each and every situation between you), you will both grow from the experience of becoming true companions. In addition, you'll have your fair share of loving and sensual moments to laugh and cry over.

His Virtues
Mr Taurus can have movie star looks and ooze charm. He will be very warm, sometimes very funny, stable, and good-natured,

and he will love to spoil you. He will help you to learn patience and he will introduce you to his hobbies—regardless of whether you want to try them or not! He can make you feel like the most important woman in the world and, once committed, he seldom strays far from home.

His Vanities

Mr Taurus often has a string of old (sometimes quite gorgeous) flames who 'stay in touch' with him. He can be as slow as molasses and as bull-headed as his zodiac symbol! If he's your soul mate, he may frustrate you enough to make you pull your hair out, and possibly his as well! He can sometimes be a bully (after all, Taurus are the bulls of the zodiac). He can be unadventurous and a stick in the mud about routine and hold old-fashioned beliefs at times.

Mr Gemini Soul Mate

It can be hard to decode whether a Gemini guy is really your soul mate or not because many of them can make a woman go weak at the knees and be quite charming and flirtatious—even when there's no soul mate connection at all.

Prepare to go on a heady adventure because you are getting the soul child, the soul boy, the soul man and the soul teacher all in one package with this guy. Because of his connection with the twins in astrology (the twins are the zodiac symbol for Geminis), this 'duality' that comes naturally to him can complicate matters—particularly when you try to decode whether he is your true soul mate or not. If you meet a Gemini man and think he is the 'one', whether he is your soul mate or not, he's going to have many levels of identity, desire, emotion and traits. He is a continuous mystery package that you are going to be constantly unwrapping to discover one new layer of personality under another!

Most Gemini men are young at heart, somewhat unreliable or irrational, and highly reactive to everything and everyone. Often he smokes, bites his nails, talks incessantly and tends to fidget, or he has other habitual pastimes such as excessive eating, drinking or playing with his computer, which he believes calms him down. This side of him is the 'soul boy' attitude. Alternatively, he can be stable, wise, reliable and less irrational, which is what I term the 'soul man' Gemini personality. After spending time with him you'll be able to see if he is the soul boy, which is the younger soul type—an individual with less incarnations on this planet from which to draw wisdom from—or the soul man, who is wiser and less reactionary to every little irritation or drama that occurs. Some Gemini men have a real mix of both, switching between the soul boy and the soul man personalities.

If he is the soul man, then your soul mate experience will be easygoing (and easier to recognise) than if he is the soul boy. This is not to say that you'll get a lesser love experience from either of these two types, just that you'll probably have to be more attentive and giving to the soul boy. Why the soul boy is often more demanding is because when it comes to the deeper and more unconscious levels of life and the soul experience, unless the Gemini you meet is a highly evolved individual, they can be the masters of mixed messages. Therefore, don't expect to really understand them and their complex make-up at all times. Indeed, even pinning them down to a long-term heart-and-soul connection may not be simple. For some reason Geminis are often 'ready to run' from very deep connections.

If you remain calm in their presence and pay special attention to the more psychic or unconscious electrical energy fields that surround us all—that is, if you tune into the unspoken and unexpressed feelings in the air—you'll discover that there is a special electrified buzz around most Gemini males. This charged energy is manifested because their nervous energy operates on overdrive most of the time. Geminis are often highly strung and extremely busy within their own thoughts. Their internal dialogue never seems to stop, even when they are sleeping! Therefore, Geminis themselves often have a problem picking up the subtle messages of the unconscious mind. The more subtle levels of operation often pass them by, because they are so busy in another place in their own thoughts. This preoccupation can also stop them from picking up messages from their heart and soul.

This fixation with their inner self, or their preoccupation with their own mind messages is why Geminis can often walk right past their soul mates or have a relationship with their true soul mate and not even tap into this potential heart and soul connection. In fact, some Geminis can have such an intense mental existence that it keeps them from having a close relationship with anybody else other than themselves, most of the time! Therefore, making a soul mate connection with them can become difficult because Gemini men (and women) are multi-dimensional and often find it hard to tune in for any ongoing period of time. Ruled in astrology by Mercury, the winged messenger of the Greek gods, Geminis have wings on their thoughts, which flap around and cause too many disruptions for them to have clarity of vision or thought. There's a wonderful expression that probably sums up this aspect of the Gemini personality perfectly: 'A Gemini needs to get out of their own way!'

However, having said all that, most Gemini men are good at relationships, but sometimes not so good at the deeper soul-connected ones. There is a great attractiveness to them as well. This 'out to party' type can be well known for his sex appeal and smooth-talking charm, so it could be easy for him to seduce you and make you think you both have a super-special soul mate connection, regardless of whether you're soul mates or not. Naturally this is not always the case, but be warned—a Gemini guy has done this 'we're soul mates' sales pitch before and this type of emotional game playing rolls easily off his tongue!

Therefore, it can be quite a challenge to work out whether a Gemini man is operating from his heart or his mind. He can talk himself in and out of anything—including the best and worst of relationships. Many men born under this sign won't listen to or trust their feelings; instead they try to analyse everything with their overactive and sometimes very confused mind. So when it comes to matching up with your

Gemini soul mate, you are looking for the person who is more comfortable operating from his spiritual heart centre and not just their mind or intellectual levels.

So how can you find out which level your Gemini man is tuned in to? Gemini males can be the chameleons of the zodiac, and just when you thought you knew what the Gemini male personality was like, you'll meet another kind of Gemini man who offers the reverse side of the spectrum. Your Gemini man may be softly spoken, prepared to listen and shy when you meet him, but then turn out to be quite extroverted once you get to know him.

Despite this, most Gemini men do have days when they are outgoing and friendly or withdrawn and distant. They can be warm and cold in a moment. They usually keep you guessing and that's why it can be hard to decipher if the Gemini man is your true mate.

Until your Gemini is truly centred and operating from a balanced inner level, they can be too scattered within themselves to be 'whole' and include you in their innermost realms of operation. Therefore they can be many things to many people, rather than one true love to their own special soul mate.

One way to tell if you have a true connection with your Gemini is to slowly lay your cards face up on the table. He is usually impatient and desires quick thrills rather than long-term challenges or obligations. If, after you slow things down, he quickly takes off for easier conquests or less challenging companions, well, good riddance! But if he sticks around or keeps coming back—even when he knows he has to work hard for your true attention or devotion—that means he's listening to a deeper message from his heart and soul and is probably planning to stay.

In many cases (unless they have really made an innermost commitment), most Geminis don't stick around for long, so you may have to test him in all kinds of ways to see if he is both committed and dedicated. However, once a Gemini man feels something or makes a commitment, he can turn into the most devoted and attentive companion. Consequently, when a Gemini man meets his true soul mate, he can be magically transformed from a flirtatious man or boy into your soul knight in shining armour. Sometimes this transformation happens overnight, and sometimes it takes a long time. Usually this guy needs a little time to adjust and explore the depth of his intensely personal feelings, and yours. He might even run away from you at first because he's an air sign and doesn't want his wings clipped—not even by his soul mate. You might have the most spectacular date of your life together and then not hear from him for days or even a week. But don't worry, if you're his soul mate, he'll be back because a Gemini has a deep desire to mate with his true love.

But be prepared. Even in a soul mate relationship, he's still likely to be changeable in nature—fickle and moody one day and charming and romantic the next. This soul mate relationship can be very challenging, but even your worst arguments will be more interesting and exciting than a night on the town with anyone else. Once that soul mate connection is made, you wouldn't swap him for any other sign of the zodiac because he is going to light up your entire existence.

His Virtues

Mr Gemini is romantic, passionate, charming and very exciting. He has lots of creative energy and he'll challenge you to
expand your mind and view the world in a different light. He
will also stretch your relationship boundaries and want you to
keep up with his busy life.

His Vanities

There may be times when you feel you are in a battle of wits
against each other. Mr Gemini can push so many emotional
buttons that he will exhaust you on some days. He can be
mischievous, irresponsible and sometimes narrow-minded,
especially if he has a jealous or unreasonable streak, and
most Geminis do! He can be wasteful with money and
sometimes dishonest.

Mr Cancer Soul Mate

Unconsciously, rather than consciously, all
Cancer men are looking for a true soul-connected, unconditional love and they won't find
any real inner peace until they reconnect with
their one and only special soul mate.

Emotions are likely to hit enormous highs and lows when
you are dealing with the Cancer man because, whether he
realises it or not, he's a romantic and sometimes more so
than you would ever expect from spending time with him.

Although you may seldom guess it from listening to him or observing his habits and routines, more than any other sign of the zodiac, the Cancer man's journey through life is driven by his innermost quest to find true love. He somehow seems to have an inner compass that is constantly drawing him in this direction, but that doesn't mean that he is wise enough to follow it. He knows there is something special to be found in the love realms of experience, not the Hollywood movie type of love, but something deeper and more significant. Unconsciously, rather than consciously, Cancer men are looking for a true soul-connected, unconditional love. That's why their connection with their mother often makes the Cancer man a great admirer of the female sex; or if his relationship with his mother soured him, it sometimes makes him a total misogynist. You will learn a lot about your Cancer man when you explore his feelings towards his mother, because this most basic level of male/female connection will reveal a lot about his feelings towards all women.

The sign of Cancer is represented by the ever-changing moon in astrology—the energy force that rules the feminine psyche, emotional changes and mood swings. The moon is also connected to the family and the mother love force. All connections with women are going to be strong influences in this man's life. He is searching within himself for his own feminine side too. No matter how well or poorly connected he is with his own mother, underneath all the superficial structures of his masks and personas, a Cancer man is a mother/goddess/soul mate love seeker. He wants to be loved more than anything else, but he will often go about this quest in a most destructive way. He will shy away from real love at times because of his low self-esteem or his inability to love himself. And here is the big clue to the Cancer man's self-development because if he doesn't love himself or feel worthy, he will always push love away. He needs to learn to love himself first in order to feel worthy of accepting love from another.

Surprisingly, even behind their macho exterior, many Cancer guys are like delicate flowers who need careful attention and nurturing to survive—at least emotionally. They are super-sensitive to other people and the outside world. That is why their zodiac symbol is so aptly the Crab. The Crab symbol reveals that they too have a form of protective shell, an armoured private world where they can retreat. In soul terms, what this Crab symbol represents is the soul living within the shell of the physical body.

Cancers, throughout their entire lives, have times when they withdraw in and out of their shells, and even as a soul mate they may not be 'there' operating on the earthly communication realms of experience for you. The Cancer man will have times when he must reconnect with his innermost soul world. However, on the soul levels of operation, in those more subtle realms of experience, your Cancer man will be more easily connected to you than the other zodiac signs.

If you've already fallen for a Cancer guy and you think he's your soul mate, tread carefully because he's going to be a man with many different sides to his character and his emotions are easily hurt. No matter how much you want to rush into his arms and tell him that you love him, or how much he means to you, don't do it until the moment is 'exactly perfect' for him! You don't need to be in a hurry either, because often the Cancer man will make the first move and express his soul love for you anyway. If you have a soul mate connection with him, be patient. If he senses a connection with you, there is a strong possibility, if handled properly and with respect, that this relationship will last forever. But be wary that you don't chase him away by being overly demanding or emotionally aggressive.

There's a fine line between winning or losing him, or pleasing or displeasing him. He does need a lot of reassurance, so if you play games or hold your feelings back too much, he'll lose confidence and be frightened off. Therefore, from the first meeting, you'll need to be very attentive to the subtle feelings in operation between you and know when to be open and when to be distant with him.

As mentioned earlier, Cancer is ruled by the moon, so to test if he is your soul mate, take a long walk with him in the light of the full moon and see what happens. If you're soul mates, you'll feel his innermost energy fields connecting with your own, and he won't be able to resist your loving feelings if you project them in his direction—even if his insecure side would rather run back into his shell. Once the soul mate connection is made with your Cancer man, he'll be a very interesting lover and you're in for some heart-pounding steamy nights. He can surprise you with some of his imaginative ideas regarding where and how to make love. Romantically, he can be very enchanting and if you're in his heart, he will cherish you and be fiercely protective of you (as

long as you never say a bad thing about him or his mother!).
He will also test your spirit and patience, and on some days
he will challenge you in every way possible. But ultimately,
your soul mate journey with him will make your heart sing
and give you the true knowledge that love can have wings
that lift you up to the stars and beyond.

His Virtues
Mr Cancer can be very understanding, charming and sensitive
and he will love taking care of you. He will help you to learn
some valuable lessons about yourself and the depth of your
emotions. He has the magic to keep you enchanted, and he's
exceptionally devoted to his soul mate.

His Vanities
Mr Cancer can be extremely contrary and relentless when he
wants his own way. He can be moody, insecure and on some
days downright crabby. He's extremely possessive at times,
and when he's depressed he can be very irrational. He can
also be close to insanely jealous (often for absolutely no
reason at all). He may expect you to love his mother or his
family as much as you love him.

Mr Leo Soul Mate

Be warned—more women have thought a Leo
man was their soul mate than any other hunky
man of the zodiac.

Join the 'Is he my soul mate?' line ahead of you! This man usually has broken many a fair maiden's heart—not intentionally, although sometimes he can be quite a harsh romantic game player, but usually because he naturally has a special kind of power over the female sex that he doesn't quite know how to control. He does seem to be able to flirt, seduce and fascinate those around him, which does turn him into heartbreak material—even when he has the best of romantic intentions. More women have thought a Leo man was their soul mate than any other hunky man of the zodiac. He's got natural soul mate qualities, because he has 'heart', and many women read his ability to be affectionate and attentive as a signpost of their true heart's connection with him. No wonder Mr Leo is ranked among the top Romeos of the zodiac! So be warned that your heart-felt feelings for Mr Leo could simply be romantic fancies. And remember that he can turn his seductive, sparkling charm on and off like a tap—his charms to make you feel so unique and special, that is.

Don't jump to conclusions when qualifying your zodiac Leo man as a potential soul mate. It may take a while to discover whether you have a soul mate connection or to learn that he is simply trying to sweep you off your feet for the fun of it. Either way, you're in for a wild ride because Mr Leo can perfectly portray the role of both the prince and the toad. So how do you find out if he's your soul mate? Play the role of the damsel in distress and not just once, because that mightn't work; you may need to play it a couple of times to see if he passes the soul mate test. A Leo male who feels a soul mate connection with you will drop practically everything to rush to your side at the slightest hint of difficulty or despair. He likes to show his courage, feel needed and protective towards his loved ones. If he doesn't feel connected to you, he'll think of a zillion excuses to avoid taking on any responsibilities or commitments where you are concerned.

When a Leo man connects (and he does this by opening up his heart to you), he can be very aggressive and seductive about getting you to make a powerful heart commitment to him. He can jump into relationships quickly, but then just as quickly disappear out of them. Always remember 'romance' is his middle name and he can be a true heartbreaker, unless he really is your soul mate (and with a Leo he can sometimes feel he is every woman's soul mate, if it suits him).

If you think your Leo is your soul mate, you have to prepare yourself for an equal share of good fortune and adversity, because he can be your greatest teacher in life but also your toughest, most unsettling critic. Remember that he is a fire sign and is accustomed to getting what he wants the way he wants it. He will also expect a great deal from you, and many of the things he expects may turn out to be very unrealistic.

This soul encounter with him and the physical, emotional, romantic and psychological journey it will propel you on will include a lot of give and take—with you doing most of the giving! There will be times when you might feel pressured to give in to his desires just to keep the peace. This can lead to all kinds of future resentments or break-ups, so it is vital for you to remain true to yourself and your dreams, if you want this relationship to form a secure, long-lasting basis. Don't sell your soul to please him! A Leo is always looking for love, but soul love is a different thing altogether and you may have to be his teacher now and again and reveal the difference between the mundane and the magnificent. You must make him meet you halfway or he could end up spoiling what otherwise could turn out to be a lifelong party for the both of you.

His Virtues

Mr Leo can be very amorous, poetic, ambitious, confident and energetic. He will be a loving mate and a fun partner who likes to share his friends and interests with you. His enthusiasm will be contagious and he can help you to reach many of your own goals, just by believing in you.

His Vanities

Mr Leo can be very proud, domineering and arrogant at times. When he's tired or frustrated, he can be very temperamental with a short fuse. He likes to order people around and that includes you, even if you're his soul mate.

Mr Virgo Soul Mate

If you have a true soul mate connection with a Virgo man, he will yearn for you for eternity, and while he waits to reconnect with you, he will feel as if a part of him is always empty or missing, and you will feel the same way too.

Expect to be asking yourself the age-old question time and again, 'He loves me, he loves me not?' if you meet a Virgo guy and think he's possibly 'the one'. If you're falling in love with a Virgo guy and wondering if he's your soul mate, watch out, because he can be the master of mixed messages! You'll need to listen to your heart and your head (and definitely not the input of friends or family) to figure out if he's a true soul mate or not. And sometimes Virgo guys can be clever romantic opportunists too. Some of the more wily Virgo men are known for being able to make women feel like soul mates, even if they're not. So, step number one is to clear your spinning head of all the dizzy romantic feelings you have for him long enough to be objective, then go away for a week to visit a friend, or stay at home and don't answer the phone. If you have a soul mate connection, he will yearn for you while you're 'gone', as if a part of him is missing, and you will feel the same way too.

Mr Virgo churns over everything in his mind time and again and sometimes thinks too much. He can turn even the simplest feelings or encounters into a major drama or big deal. He can concern himself over things that may or may not ever happen. He can turn his stomach into a knot of angst simply by worrying about what colour tie to wear, so imagine what he can put himself through when it comes to choosing the love of his life! Therefore, if he is deeply affected by the encounter he has had with you, or the fact that the relationship between you is intensifying, this may work against him growing close to you. In fact, it may encourage him to put up some rather powerful barriers against you. Indeed, you may have a romantic chase ahead of you, or some kind of test of patience to pass before he allows you to step over the threshold of his vulnerable outlook into the loving chambers of his heart. He isn't likely to be easy-going—quite the opposite, in fact. Being perfectionists and very selective about who they get involved with, Virgos shy away from early commitment. But if he's your soul mate, then he won't want to let you get away, even if he doesn't openly show it at first. He may not even realise the bond you two have until you're out of touch for a while.

For many a Virgo man, you need to 'treat them mean to keep them keen'. It may not work every time, but it is often very revealing. And be aware that absence will only make his heart grow fonder if you are soul mates. If not, absence will put out the romantic fires completely and he will resent you, forget you, or replace you and possibly even insult you...rather than honour and praise you. If he thinks you are his soul mate, he will love you for your imperfections. If he doesn't love you for your imperfections, he will tell you all the time what's wrong with you, so it will be easy (once the relationship is more in flow) to know how deep his love goes for you. If he constantly talks about your need to diet, change your hair colour or complains about your dress sense, he is obviously very superficially connected and not soul connected.

When a Virgo man makes a true soul mate connection, he is often completely charmed, becomes very single-minded and forgets about his other responsibilities. Part of his soul mate's role is to help keep him on track in his own life, even though he tends to resist it. This creates some sparks and even some heated arguments. This soul journey isn't meant to be easy, but it is sure to be very exciting and incredibly fulfilling.

His Virtues
Mr Virgo is dependable, punctual, sincere, practical, deliberate and very sexy in a serious sort of way. He has lots of self-discipline and will support you in your efforts for self-improvement. He'll also be willing to put time and effort into keeping your relationship in top soul mate condition!

His Vanities
Mr Virgo can be quick to notice faults in everyone, including himself, and he can hand out some very insensitive criticism. He worries a lot and has a great deal of tension knotting up in his muscles, but he won't admit it. His perfectionism can be unbearable and is sure to drive you batty every once in a while.

Mr Libra Soul Mate

If you're in a relationship with a Libra man, then there's a very good chance you will feel a soul mate connection with him long before he acknowledges it himself.

Uh oh! You are going to be put through the relationship wringer with this guy. A soul mate connection with a Libra man can be one of the most incredible yet frustrating relationships in the zodiac because even though Librans have a deep desire to share their love with a soul mate, few of them will admit it to themselves or to you for that matter!

Aside from the fact that Librans—as a sign—are notoriously and agonisingly slow at making their minds up, some Libra men are so caught up in themselves (to see what I mean, just check whether he watches his reflection in a window as he walks down the street), that many wouldn't know their soul mate even if they were married to them! If you're in a relationship with a Libra man, there's a very good chance you will feel a soul mate connection with him long before he's able to acknowledge it himself. He's a charmer, he's a lover and he's usually a hunk too; but he's also a ditherer and spends a great deal of his time 'fence sitting'. He's also great at playing mind games and his fear of intimacy, rejection or being taken for a romantic ride can stand in the way of him trusting his heart, especially when it comes to making a soul mate commitment. This is a guy who finds it much easier to talk about love, rather than experience it for himself firsthand.

As an air sign, Libra guys (especially if they are into socialising) often drift from one relationship to the next in order to avoid getting attached to any one woman. It is as if the very thing they want the most—an intense soul mate connection—is the very thing they run away from, the second no one's looking. Then, of course, there's the Libra man's tendency to lead women on—even if he knows in his heart that she isn't his soul mate. In their defence, however, this caddish behaviour stems from a misguided attempt at kindness. Warm-hearted, Libran men can find themselves in all manner of relationship hot spots when their pure intentions are misinterpreted as something more meaningful.

To determine Mr Libra's true soul mate potential, you'll need to stay one step ahead of him at all times. The ultimate soul mate test, however, is to invite him to a quiet family dinner with your parents. He will make any excuse to avoid this invitation *unless* he feels a connection with you on a deeper soul level (or if your parents are super-rich). If he says yes, he's being guided by his soul, rather than his fears! If your Libra man passes this 'meet the folks' test, you can look forward to some amazing times together because when he meets his true other half and recognises the bond he has with her, he's in seventh heaven and prepared to make any sacrifice necessary to ensure the two of you stay together.

Now while this may not keep him faithful (because Mr Libra is often distracted by 'the grass is greener' syndrome), true soul mate love creates the cosmic musical harmony he needs to function at his highest level, and he'll pull out all the stops to charm you. Keep in mind, though, that he's ruled by Venus—the 'love them or leave them' planet, and that means even if you're soul mates, he can still be very fickle in expressing his affections, and there will be times when you wonder if he loves you at all. You will need to learn a great deal of patience to enjoy this soul mate connection, and you will need to take the bad with the good on this soul journey.

His Virtues

Mr Libra's social scene and his extensive easygoing nature and popularity can make him a great guy to be around. He can be gorgeous, absolutely charming, very diplomatic, affectionate and sympathetic. He is a good listener and will be more than willing to help you solve problems. He will value your soul mate relationship and be happy to spend the rest of his life with you.

His Vanities

Selfish can take on a whole new meaning where Mr Libra is concerned. His world can revolve around him, him and only him. He can be lazy, indulgent and extremely frustrating to be around. At times he's downright nasty and he may expect to be waited on hand and foot. He can also be childishly petty and vain.

Mr Scorpio Soul Mate

If you're falling under the special love spell of a Scorpio man, don't wait another day to test your soul mate connection to see whether he is your special soul mate. He's worth the time and energy you are putting into him, because this guy can be the most magnetic and serious heartbreaker on the planet.

If you think a Scorpio man is your potential soul mate, you've got a very intense journey of the heart, mind and body ahead of you. Mr Scorpio is no open book. He's deep, brooding and secretive (especially about his emotions, passions and desires). He's the zodiac male who is constantly battling himself, learning the difference between what he values the most—the love of power, or the power of love. If you're falling under the spell of a Scorpio man, don't wait another day to test your soul mate connection because this guy can be the most magnetic and serious heartbreaker on the planet. He has a powerful ability to bewitch his romantic partners and have them fall under the power of his sexual, charming, hypnotic spell. But just because he can have a profound effect upon you doesn't mean he has serious or long-term intentions! He can turn on the psychic love con- nection power that comes naturally to him when and where he wants to use it, and then just as quickly he can decide to switch it off! When a Scorpio man has had enough of his time with you or he detects something in a partner that isn't compatible with his idea of a soul mate, he steps out for a cup of coffee and doesn't come back.

The best way to determine if your Scorpio man is a soul mate is to test his level of trust. Put him in a position where you know he has a chance to flirt behind your back (such as leaving him alone with one of your gorgeous girlfriends) and see if he plays the heel or not. If he doesn't value his con- nection to you, rest assured he'll be off like a rocket.

The Scorpio male has a tough time trusting people, and not even his closest friends escape his distrust and suspi- cions. If he really loves you, he needs to trust you too. And, of course, you need to be able to trust him as well. He needs to feel that you are a cosmic soul team and are building up a connection of value, otherwise Scorpio's can just be a 'soul mate pretender' and there are many of these around.

If he passes this test, it's very possible you're soul connected, but don't kid yourself about living happily ever after because this guy will push all your emotional buttons. For one thing he loves power, and even if you've been dominant in other relationships, you'll rarely succeed in wielding any influence over a Scorpio man. To make this soul journey a success story, you'll need to remember that you're both separate people with your own ideas and values. This relationship can teach you more about yourself than you may want to learn, but ultimately you will receive the rich reward of true soul fulfilment. If you're his soul mate, you're in for the most exciting and volatile time of your life.

His Virtues

Mr Scorpio can be incredibly sexy, very perceptive and imaginative, and profoundly sensitive. His inner energy and power are infinite and he is just as interested in helping his soul mate to accomplish her goals as he is in achieving his own. He will be the most protective, faithful and dedicated partner, if he really has a special connection with you.

His Vanities

Mr Scorpio won't show any sign of weakness and hates anyone to hold any type of power over him. Controlling others and his environment really means the difference between him feeling weak or strong. He can be annoyingly secretive about his business dealings, and almost impossible to influence. He does what he wants to do, when he wants to do it, and while you might think this is a direct affront to you, it isn't. It's simply the Scorpio way, whether you're his soul mate or not.

Mr Sagittarius Soul Mate

Like parts of a cosmic puzzle falling neatly into place, when a Sagittarius guy comes to the realisation that he's met his soul mate, it can be amazing how magically all the other parts of his life begin to come together as well.

Shooting stars may light the sky, bells may chime, rainbows may fill the air and flowers might suddenly blossom wherever you two are standing—all these things and more can occur when you meet a Sagittarius man who is your special true love. But even if it rains down rose petals, don't expect Mr Sagittarius to notice! In fact, you may have to tell your Sagittarian that the two of you have a soul mate connection (or hint at it, so he can't fail to notice), because he's probably shooting his energy out in a hundred directions and so caught up in his own swirl of hyperactivity, that even if he feels a deep connection with you, it might not occur to him that you are his true mate.

As one of the most forthright signs of the zodiac, the best way to test your possible soul mate connection is to be very direct and brutally honest. Write him a loving letter telling him exactly how you feel, and if he responds favourably, then with some kind of magical tact, delicately ask him to marry you. If it all sounds rather forward, don't panic—your Sagittarius man is all for getting things out into the open. Besides, not known for their sensitivity to life's subtler nuances, most Sagittarius men won't reach this point in their relationship without some help and a little gentle prodding. He's the man who is possibly too busy to smell the roses or see the sunset, unless you point it out to him and when you do, he'll be eternally grateful that you did.

When a Sagittarius guy comes to the realisation that he's met his soul mate, it can be amazing how magically all the other parts of his life begin to come together as well—and this won't go by unnoticed. The positive effect that you have on his life will ensure you are treated as a true equal, with valuable ideas, opinions and advice. Having said that however, your Sagittarius mate won't necessarily share your opinions or give up his own ideas, and he will remain very much his own person. Your soul mate connection will give you the inside track in his life, but he will always be the one directing his own decisions—or at least the major ones. On this count, he can be one of the most frustrating males of the zodiac to deal with, simply because he always thinks that he is so easygoing and laid back—when the truth is, he isn't at all! Behind his happy-go-lucky approach to life is a much more organised, structured and conservative personality than anyone would ever guess.

If you meet a Sagittarius man and think he is your soul mate, remember that he's a fire sign, which means his mind is always racing into the future, and his passion for what he believes in comes before everything else in his life—including you at times. You will need to compromise and allow him his freedom, and give him the space to create and build his dreams (whether they be castles in the sky or real earthly structures), or the two of you will be forever at each other's throats! A soul mate connection with a Sagittarian can be sheer bliss one day and true hell the next, but your soul journey is guaranteed to bring out your best and most inspired love for each other if you persevere. Once you both commit to each other and trust and dedication is formed between you, this relationship can turn into one of the most romantic soul mate and character building encounters of all.

His Virtues

Mr Sagittarius can be dashingly confident and certain, very energetic, and usually ambitious. His curiosity and enthusiasm is contagious and he will treat you with all the love and respect a soul mate relationship inspires. He'll believe in you and in your dreams, and he'll help you to make your most heartfelt wishes come true. He will be kind, considerate and generous (usually!).

His Vanities

Mr Sagittarius can be a bit much at times and sometimes his ego is insufferable! He can be impatient, impulsive and brutally honest, and there are times when he's so focused on himself that you may wonder if he remembers you're in this together. He only has one way of doing things and that's 'his way', even though he may pretend that he will accommodate other people's plans, usually he ends up doing his own 'thing' anyway.

Mr Capricorn Soul Mate

If a Capricorn guy is your true soul mate, at your initial physical contact (even with the brush of skin on your arms), the earth may seem to move beneath your feet—and when your eyes first meet, you could suddenly become tongue-tied or forget what you were about to say.

Technicolour flashes may race through your mind, transporting you back into past lives when you meet your soul mate and he is born under the sign of Capricorn. On all kinds of psychic, dream or consciousness levels there can definitely be a touch of déjà vu surrounding the events that unfold in this relationship. In fact, a flash of recognition that makes you feel like you've known each other for a very long time, even if you have just met, sometimes sparks this soul mate connection. If your Capricorn man is truly your soul mate, you're likely to feel very comfortable with him, but the energy between you will be so strong that when your eyes meet, you could become tongue-tied or forget what you were about to say. Once you regain your balance, to test if you truly have a soul mate connection, leave him a message, make a request of him or arrange to do something special with him and see how quickly he responds.

Capricorn guys are very practical and goal-oriented, so his response time will show you how high you are on his priority list. If you hear from him within a day, you can bet you're important to him, and there's a great chance the two of you are already connected. However, not hearing from him doesn't mean that he isn't 'the one'—it could just indicate that you have some hard work ahead of you, before he is likely to appreciate the fact that you have met each other.

However, you may not need to have any apprehensions about the potential that this man is your soul mate. When a Capricorn man's soul connects, he usually feels it right away, even if he doesn't tell you for a long time. You may need to read between the lines in your communications with him, rather than expect everything to be out into the open between you. He can, in fact, be scared off if you quickly bring up that fact that you fit together like two pieces of a magical puzzle. Remember he's an earth sign, so he's patient and willing to take his time savouring your romantic friendship, instead of rushing recklessly forward. He's a knight of the old code, and if he is your soul mate, his heart will always be true. He may not want to rush into anything before he has tested the strength of his feelings on all kinds of everyday levels of operation.

If you think you have met your soul mate, and he is a Capricorn (and he feels the same way about your relationship), prepare yourself for a bittersweet lifetime of unconditional love. This soul mate journey will take you to the height of joy and pleasure and drop you to the depths of heartache and longing. But if he is your soul mate, everything that occurs between you is part of your destiny together and will open your heart to a new way of living and loving. A relationship with a Capricorn man that has soul mate potential is likely to be one of the most rewarding, long-lasting and highly productive relationships of the zodiac.

His Virtues
Mr Capricorn can be loyal, honest and very honourable. He will encourage you to explore new ideas and consider new ways of looking at life and relationships. He has the clever wit to keep you smiling and laughing, and his magnetic energy will keep you very warm. He is a solid anchor in your life and he will not let you down when the going gets tough.

His Vanities
Sometimes Mr Capricorn can be extremely one-eyed about what is right or wrong. In fact, he can play judge and jury over everybody else's lives, without realising he is passing judgment upon them. He can be too practical for his own good sometimes and he's rarely willing to make a spur of the moment decision or take a spontaneous step. He can be depressed for days and he's usually lazy when it comes to housework.

Mr Aquarius Soul Mate

If you have a soul mate connection with your special Aquarius guy, you'll feel an overwhelming sense of oneness with him like you've never felt before.

Expect to feel all kinds of psychic shock waves hurtling around you if you connect with the special energy of your soul mate and he is born under the zodiac sign of Aquarius. This man, if he is your other half, will take you on one of the more mind-blowing romantic experiences of the zodiac. This soul mate connection can knock you right off your feet and make the rest of the world disappear. Most people feel an immediate bond with Aquarius males, but if you have a special bond with your Aquarian, you'll feel an overwhelming sense of oneness with him like you've never felt before. When Mr Aquarius holds your hand, it will seem so familiar that you might feel like you're holding your own hand. Sometimes you will both say the same thing at the same time. And best of all, you will often find that you can spend hours in each other's company without even needing to talk to each other. There's a quiet confident energy around you that provides the freedom to spend time together without needing to communicate on everyday levels. You do not need words to 'sense' the closeness between you—the link that exists subliminally is like an invisible cosmic electricity that sizzles and connects you to each other's mind, body and spirit.

To test if your Aquarius man is your true soul mate, find out how deeply you understand him. Most Aquarius guys are desperately seeking a mate who understands them, because they are one of the most misunderstood masculine signs of the zodiac. If you're soul connected, you could be the first person on this planet that somehow understands him—and he will love you greatly for this ability to feel and sense his true meanings and thoughts. If you are truly connected, you'll understand his deeper beliefs and philosophies about life, and he'll realise his soul mate has finally arrived! Another way of explaining this is, when he talks to you, you'll intuitively sense and really know what he is talking about—when others are left in the dark.

If you think your Aquarius man is your soul mate, you may feel as if you're under some sort of spell—one that gives you an exclusive connection to each other. As much as this is true, you are exclusively and cosmically connected to each other as potential soul mates. Nevertheless, it would still be a good idea to widen your view to see all the other people who are a big part of his life. You should also be close to his friends or pets. He's an air sign, so even if you're his soul mate, he won't necessarily live his life around you. He has a lot of friends and meets new ones all the time, so if you're the possessive or jealous type, this relationship may some-times push your patience and make you feel vulnerable well beyond anything you've ever experienced before. Even when an Aquarius man knows he's met his soul mate, he won't be in any hurry to make it official, and if you pressure him, you could push him away.

When an Aquarius soul connects, a deep void within him is filled and he will look as if a big weight has been lifted from his shoulders and his eyes twinkle with the joy of true love. This soul mate journey can be one of the most rewarding, providing you allow him his space and are honest about your needs and desires. You can count on some rough times together, but as long as you communicate openly, you can triumph over any difficulties that may arise.

His Virtues

Mr Aquarius can be innovative, caring and humane. He's tolerant and will respect your opinions, even if he doesn't agree with them. His charismatic personality will pull all sorts of characters and opportunities into your life together and you will both grow in leaps and bounds from this journey. He can be very honourable.

His Vanities

Mr Aquarius loves his independence and the thing he values most is his 'thinking space'. He can be very scattered, eccentric and detached and there's a good chance he'll forget important occasions like your birthday or anniversary. He's a drifter of sorts and it may be nearly impossible to pin him down or get a definitive answer about anything.

Mr Pisces Soul Mate

Fate often lends a hand or destiny plays a significant role in creating the way you meet your Pisces soul mate.

Prepare to have stars in your eyes and difficulty keeping both feet firmly on the ground. You are entering the realm of romantic fantasy when you embark on a relationship with a Pisces man. Nothing is likely to be ordinary or commonplace about the exchanges that occur between you—and this applies to both the positive and negative effects of all encounters—as life is certain to have many ups and downs once you two have met and have decided to become a couple.

Fate often lends a hand or destiny plays a significant role when it comes to how you meet your Pisces soul mate. This serendipitous connection is strongly noticeable because he is a man born under the ethereal, mystical sign of Pisces. If your actual introduction or first meeting isn't one of those spine-tingling experiences (which will often be the case), before too long has passed, it's likely that something amazing will suddenly occur, something that will make you realise that he has the potential to be your special soul mate. You may get to know each other through an accident, a blind date, a computer introduction service or some freaky kind of incident. Or this soul mate connection may begin in a work environment or the synchronicity of travelling at the same time and being seated together. Yet no matter how it unfolds or presents itself, before you know it, once the love spell hits, you're drifting down the river of dreams together and floating on cloud nine. If he's had a lot of very close and meaningful relationships (and many Pisces men have trouble with monogamous relationships), you need to remember that, despite the above, he may not be your *real* soul mate because Pisces guys seem to 'think' someone is their soul mate more than any other sign of the zodiac. But if you know a Pisces man whom you think may be your soul mate, there are definitely a few quick and helpful ways to find out.

One of the best ways is to spend a few days together in a secluded place. It is important to have an intimate time together to delve into the depths of your Pisces man's mind, imagination, hopes, dreams and wishes. So do whatever you can to create an ivory tower experience. Block out the world, exclude the company of others, and separate yourself from any distractions or outside interference including the television, radio and telephone. What you are looking to accomplish in this quality time together is the opportunity to share your most inspired thoughts and dreams with your Pisces man. If you have a soul mate connection, he will get tears in his eyes when you reveal your innermost secrets, dreams and wishes to him, and you will get tears in your eyes when he does the same. You should also be able to 'feel' each other's moods and 'sense' each other's thoughts, without actually physically expressing them. The soul and psychic connections are usually strong between the Pisces man and his soul mate and it is even possible that you have dreamt of each other or had visions of each other before meeting.

When a Pisces guy feels a deep soul mate connection, being one of the more psychically driven star signs, he can become completely immersed in the relationship and in his soul partner. But remember that he is a water sign, so you don't want him to become 'unhealthily' dependent upon the relationship. Whether you are true soul mates or not, he still needs to keep in touch with the real world too. Although he will always feel this closeness to you, at some point he will need to invite the rest of the world back into his life. This doesn't mean he's losing interest in you or your connection to him; it just means he's being himself. If you think your Pisces man is your soul mate, this is the perfect opportunity to cultivate your patience and trust (and there are likely to be times when they will be tested).

If you believe that you are in a relationship with a Pisces man who is your soul mate, you're on a very interesting journey. Remember that he's very sensitive and rarely aggressive, even if you want him to be. It will be up to you to fan the flames of your romance and reassure him that you love him and want to stay in his life. You can expect some slow periods in your relationship and possibly some times when you feel more like friends than lovers, but you can rekindle the passion if you try, and the deeper your friendship, the deeper your love will ultimately grow.

His Virtues
Mr Pisces has magic at his fingertips and he'll introduce you to new ways of living, loving and sharing. He is one of the least judgmental and most compassionate signs of the zodiac. He can be sweet, kind and poetic, and he will be very sympathetic to your needs and desires. Together, you can reach a level of intimacy that few couples, even soul mates, ever reach.

His Vanities
Mr Pisces is often tempted to take the easy or escapist road, and is willing to resign himself to his circumstances, instead of putting some effort into changing his course. He can act like the most pathetic victim, and he may even blame you, on occasion, for his troubles. He often sees bad habits as harmless, innocent fun...even when they are very unwise actions or dangerous risks for him to take.

Star Gals
Ms Aries Soul Mate

This soul mate connection often begins like a roller-coaster racing through the Tunnel of Love, complete with all the thrilling hills, unexpected curves and even some butterflies churning in your stomach!

Hold onto your heartstrings and tightly fasten your emotional seatbelt—if Ms Aries is your possible soul mate then you should be well prepared to go on a wild ride. You are about to experience many speed bumps along the emotional pathway of life if you intend to find out if Ms Aries is your soul mate. This soul mate connection often begins like a roller-coaster racing through the Tunnel of Love, complete with all the thrilling hills, unexpected curves and even some butterflies churning in your stomach! When the romantic and intoxicating effects of this attraction slows down, to test if she is your soul mate, take her on a secluded weekend getaway where there's nothing to do but to get to know each other better. If she's your soul mate, she'll be enchanted by your romantic plans, but if she's not, she'll be bored, restless and may even suggest you cut the weekend short. She may even throw a tizzy-fit over nothing before you've known her very long. Expect her to be overly dramatic and less sensitive to your emotional needs, desires or wishes—if she is not your soul mate.

And whether or not she is your soul mate, don't expect this relationship to flow smoothly or to be easy to judge. Ms Aries is a zodiac gal who runs either super-hot or super-cold—she can often drive you close to distraction when she swings one way and then the other in rapid succession. And even when an Aries girl's soul connects, she may not admit it to herself that she has met her special man. Denial, particularly regarding her emotions, can be a big part of this gal's personality. She's a spontaneous free spirit and even though she may think she is looking for love and is eager to settle down with her true soul mate, the word 'commitment' can still make her cringe. But if she is secure within herself (often a rare occurrence for Ms Aries, but it does and can happen), and once she accepts her heartfelt connection with her soul mate, she'll shower you with love, support and attention. But beware, because she can be so intense, if you're not her true soul mate, her love and enthusiasm can smother you. Ms Aries can and will go to great extremes to either make life easy for you or complicate your existence. The Aries woman's determination, strong will, and head-strong attitude to life can work both for and against you at times. In relationships, this fiery nature often works against you, whereas in dealing with the pressures of life, it can provide the passion and enthusiasm needed to overcome any obstacle or to defeat any competitor or opposition.

If you think Ms Aries is your soul mate, keep in mind that she's a fire sign and her moody temperamental nature is scorchingly hot at times. She's an all-or-nothing kind of gal and this soul mate relationship is sure to push some of your most sensitive buttons, and possibly scare her as well. Ms Aries doesn't like to feel out of control or find herself trapped within the power of someone else's moods, whims or wishes (which only drive her all over the place with their tenacious tugs and pulls at her heart, mind and body). But being charged up and volatile in nature is the way she'll help you to grow and her passion will be every bit as hot as her anger. She's one of the most sensuous ladies of the zodiac, so this is sure to be a very exciting soul mate match-up and one that will either sizzle and succeed, or sizzle and burn out.

Her Virtues
Ms Aries is a great gal pal, playmate and a wonderful lover. You won't be bored around her, as she will be very energetic and action-oriented. She's a bit of a tomboy and she'll have fun joining in with you on some of your favourite 'guy things'. She loves to try new and novel activities of all sorts and she's a great friend and travelling companion. She will believe in you and support you in your dreams.

Her Vanities
Ms Aries is competitive and may not like you to take the lead or be too opinionated (however she loves to speak her mind!). She can be restless and impatient and can pace around the room like a caged animal if she doesn't burn up all her energy. She can be very jealous and possessive, but she won't accept these qualities in you. She has a talent for exaggerating and it can be hard to know when she's telling the truth and when she's weaving a fantasy.

Ms Taurus Soul Mate

> If you're soul mates with a Taurus gal, you'll gladly take the bad with the good, and you won't be able to imagine life with anyone but her.

Prepare to face a test! Acknowledging that you and your Taurus gal are possible soul mates can be a slow process and it may take time for your relationship to develop. Being born under an earth sign, Ms Taurus is naturally level-headed and cautious. Usually a Taurus gal likes to take her time about life and love and the way she moves into long-term relationships is no exception to this 'don't rush into the unknown before you check it out' rule. So if you think the Taurus lady in your life is your soul mate, you may need to be patient and persistent to find out for sure.

This is one of the zodiac gals who doesn't blithely hand over her trust, loyalty, future plans or heart to just anyone. You'll probably have to wait until you've invested some time and energy in developing your friendship with her and deservedly earning her respect (time and again) before you can get close enough to her heart to decode if she's your true soul mate. This is one gal who cannot be hurried because it isn't part of her nature. She isn't someone who is prepared to take short cuts and she rarely takes speedy leaps of faith. This gal will prefer you to play the suitor, friend, mentor, playmate and companion before she will allow you to assume the possible mantle of soul mate. However, there are exceptions to this.

If you both have a truly unique electric soul mate connection, you may not have to do the soul mate test, but you'll need to come up with something magical that totally blows her off her sturdy earth gal feet to have her acknowledge your special connection with her. This won't be easy because it will take a strong and mighty cosmic blast of soul love and a major case of déjà vu to make her sit up and take notice of your undeniable cosmic connection.

So assuming that you two have hit it off enough to feel there is something 'very special' between you, then you can move onto the next level of trying to see if she truly has a soul mate link with you. Once you know she's comfortable with you, take her out for a gourmet dinner and arrange with the restaurant to bring her dessert with one candle on top. Tell her you've been granted one wish and you're giving it to her, but she must tell you what it is. If you're her soul mate, she'll be delighted with your creative surprise and you will be part of her wish. But if she gets a far away look in her eyes and wishes for something else entirely (something with no reference at all to you), well then, she's probably not your true mate.

Why this test works is because a Taurus gal can be very possessive when she makes a commitment. So when a Taurus lady makes a soul mate connection, she can be very single-minded about it and lose interest in many of the other aspects of her life—at least temporarily. So if you are her soul mate, her wish should include you in some fashion. This gal is ruled by the planet of love, Venus, and that is why she loves 'love' and when she meets her soul mate, one of her life's most treasured dreams comes true. But although she may be ruled by Venus, don't think that having a Taurus gal as your soul mate ensures that the rest of your life is destined for smooth sailing. This may forge a strong link between you but if she's your soul mate, she can really get under your skin too. And she is certain to be stubborn enough to make you pull your hair out at times! She's an earth sign so she can dig in her heels and refuse to budge on some issues, and she can charge recklessly ahead with other ideas. But if you're soul mates, you'll gladly take the bad with the good, and you won't be able to imagine life with anyone but her.

Her Virtues

Ms Taurus is very patient, accommodating and nurturing. She can often be willing to put your needs and desires before her own, and she will enjoy taking care of you, pampering you, and letting you know that you're number one. She will be a great companion and is also likely to keep a lovely home, be a good cook, and a terrific mother (if those things appeal to you!).

Her Vanities

Ms Taurus can be as stubborn as a bull (which is the animal symbol for her sign) and stamp her feet when she gets mad and huff and puff a lot when things do not go her way. She can be disturbingly unpunctual and will have a hard time understanding if you get angry with her about her tardiness. She's nearly impossible to push or prod in any direction she doesn't freely choose to go and pressuring her will most likely backfire every time!

Ms Gemini Soul Mate

When a Gemini woman meets the guy who may turn out to be her soul mate, she acts very strangely indeed. She is often both happy and sad at the same time because she is confounded with the range of mixed emotions she is feeling.

If you're in a relationship with a Gemini gal who you think might be your soul mate, batten down your psychological hatches because you're heading towards experiencing some head-spinning times. Ms Gemini is known for her dual nature and can be the queen of sending out mixed messages. When she says 'yes' she also shakes her head and says 'no' at the same time. She probably spends more time analysing her feelings and arguing with herself internally than any other gal in the zodiac, so even when she feels totally drawn towards you, a part of her is also attempting to pull her in the opposite direction, so she can move away from you. What is she afraid of when she tries to move away from you? Getting in over her head! She doesn't want to lose herself in her feelings and, naturally, by meeting a potential soul mate, that is exactly what happens!

If you two have really felt the sparks fly (and you probably will if there is a soul mate connection), the way to test if you have a real bond with this Gemini gal is to appeal to her mind and her heart at the same time. That way, you can charm both sides of her dualistic nature. So how do you do this? Play a game. Give her a puzzle or put her to some kind of challenge or test. For example, create a treasure hunt complete with written clues and prizes along the way that lead her to a romantic evening with you as the final treasure. If she's charmed by your creative idea and effort, and if she's starry-eyed when she discovers her treasure is you, she's the one you've been waiting for. But if she looks like a child who didn't get their favourite toy for Christmas, you can be fairly certain she's not 'the one'. Some Gemini gals can be superficial and get caught up in material things rather than soul-inspired rewards. If she is still so 'stuck' on the material levels of life, she may not see the diamond of soul light you are offering her, because she is too busy looking for the diamond to wear on her finger.

Meeting you can also turn her world upside down, and she usually doesn't know how to handle the myriad feelings she is experiencing. When a Gemini woman makes a soul mate connection (or meets someone who might be her soul mate), she is often happy and sad at the same time. She's an air sign and she's also the twin sign of the zodiac, so she understands that pain and pleasure and elation and depression are two sides of the same coin. If, after you've met and experienced a strong connection, she is sad, teary or somehow distant, please don't misinterpret her melancholy moments as sorrow or disappointment. This gal doesn't like to be overwhelmed, so if she's highly strung or peculiar for a while, give her some space. She's just balancing her emotions and trying to keep her sense of logic in the driver's seat.

This particular gal of the zodiac is an extremely complex being, so if you think you've met your soul mate and she is a Gemini, you're in for one of the most rewarding and frustrating soul mate journeys of the zodiac. You can expect lots of laughter and plenty of tears because Gemini gals are born to express both sides of themselves and when they do, they'll bring out the best and the worst in you too.

Her Virtues
The word 'adorable' takes on a higher meaning when it is used to describe the attractive qualities of the Gemini woman. She will be playful, dedicated and sensitive to your emotions and needs. She will encourage you to follow your head and your heart and show you how to master this balancing act with polish and finesse.

Her Vanities
The saying, 'Mary, Mary quite contrary', was written with her in mind. Ms Gemini can change her mind from one minute to the next and her heart can open and close so quickly you might feel like you're trapped in a revolving door, never knowing for sure if you should move forward with her, or step back.

Ms Cancer Soul Mate

When a Cancer gal believes that she has made a soul mate connection with her karmic other half, her eyes shine more brightly, her energy levels shoot up, and she smiles with every secret thought she has of her true love.

If you've met a gal and you're already feeling 'bewitched, bothered and bewildered', you are probably operating under the feminine aura of one of the most intoxicating women of the zodiac—the Cancer woman. Matching up with a Cancer woman (whether she is your soul mate or not), can be one of the most intense soul mate connections of the zodiac. If you think Ms Cancer is your soul mate, then there's a good chance you're already under her powerful magic spell. She is one woman who runs on her emotions and she either flies to the moon on her emotional highs, or crashes and burns into the depths of despair when dismay or a broken heart churns her emotions. So it is definitely wise not to play romantic games with this particular woman. Be warned to tread warily here, because disappointment weighs heavily on her gossamer wings and if you do break her heart, or run her around the romantic bush, the consequences of your actions may go far beyond your wildest imaginations. Real disaster could result.

If you really feel that you have something magical together (and you intend to follow this magical soul link through to a positive conclusion), you are ready to see if she feels the same way towards you. To test if she is your true soul mate, you'll need to open up your heart to her. Tell her you love her and you need her and see how she responds. If she's your other half, she'll want you to need her and she'll glow with the warmth of knowing how important she is to you. But if she's not your soul mate, she'll practically fade out or seem to physically disappear before your eyes. Cancer women are very sensitive to the mention of 'love'; if they think you are out of line or fooling around in any way, you could end up in big trouble. But if she believes in you and senses your heart-felt sincerity, she will either melt down with tenderness or freeze up with distaste if your attentions aren't appreciated or she doubts you.

When a Cancer gal makes a soul mate connection, her eyes shine more brightly, her energy levels shoot up, and she smiles with the thought of her true love. But that's not all. Cancer gals can be outrageously possessive of their loved ones, and she'll keep a tight grasp on you no matter how near or far away you are from each other.

If you think Ms Cancer is your soul mate, do remember that she's a water sign and ruled by the moon. This combination makes her one of the most sensitive and sometimes wishy-washy women of the zodiac. You will need to learn how to read her moods and interpret the many different looks in her eyes, or you will be in a constant state of confusion. This soul journey will take you to the moon without a rocket on some days, but on other days you may feel like you're lost in space! But if she's your soul mate, you won't want to trade her for the world, or any other planet for that matter!

Her Virtues

Ms Cancer is feminine and very mystical. She will be sensuous, sensitive and very sexy. She will show you an entirely different way to look at life and yourself and every day with her will be a new adventure and lesson in love. She has enough charm to make you smile, even in the midst of a crisis, and she is guaranteed to be true to herself and to you.

Her Vanities

Ms Cancer's moods swing back and forth so quickly that sometimes you'll feel like you're riding a pendulum through sunshine and storms. She won't tolerate rude behaviour or mistreatment from anyone under any circumstances and she won't hesitate to make a scene when she sees fit.

Ms Leo Soul Mate

The lady lion often likes and is attracted to all types of men, so it will take some extra effort to determine if the Ms Leo you know is your true soul mate or not.

So you think a Leo gal is your possible soul mate? Well, before you go anywhere further with this matter, just think of the many faces of the performer Madonna (who is a Leo) and, as obscure as it is thinking about Madonna as your own soul mate, just realise that handling any Leo gal probably won't be an easy task for any guy. You have to have a strong heart, a secure ego, and be something of a lion tamer to deal with the ferocious, feminine wiles of the Leo woman. And even if your Leo gal seems like a cuddly little pussycat at times, you should appreciate that you have a surprise package in your Leo gal and she will be a handful to deal with.

The lady lion often likes and is attracted to all types of men, so it will take some extra effort to determine if the Ms Leo you know is your true soul mate or not. This soul mate connection can be a tricky one to test because Ms Leo may treat you like a king regardless of whether she's your queen or not. To test if she's your soul mate, find out if she's willing to give you preference over her other friends or activities—just once. Call her on a night you know she has other plans and tell her you miss her and can't bear to spend the evening without her. If she reschedules her other activities or invites you to go along with her, you have a very special place in her heart and you are probably soul connected. Of course, it wouldn't be a good idea to make a habit of this, because no matter how much she loves you, she will continue to maintain a life of her own.

Once she's made a connection with her soul mate, Ms Leo can be so enthusiastic and intense that you might feel overwhelmed at times. She'll shower you with special gifts, romantic surprises and unexpected pleasures, but her attention and affection do have some strings attached. She will expect her soul mate to openly show his appreciation and freely express his love and admiration. If you don't respond as she wishes, you are sure to encounter her other side, which can be testy, cold and arrogantly distant.

If you think you've met your soul mate and she is a Leo, do remember that she's a fire sign and that means she's an action person and doesn't like to sit around waiting for things to happen. She wants you to get up and get moving. She won't let you mess her life up or deal her any short straws either. She's not likely to settle for second best in any area of life (at least not for long, anyway), particularly her relationship with you. This soul journey will stretch you beyond your current limits and force you to jump hurdles and sidestep roadblocks as a matter of course. You'll need to come up with 'trumps' time and again to prove your love is true. But that's precisely what makes this soul mate connection so rewarding and exciting. A Leo woman can take you further than you ever dreamed you could go, and if you pass her many tests, she will give you loyalty, fidelity, affection and trust—all gift wrapped in an abundance of soul love.

Her Virtues
Ms Leo is a natural entrepreneur and has a tremendous will and drive to attain high results. She is self-motivated, energetic and bright. She will be a loyal mate and will quickly become your best and most valued friend and confidante. Her passion is unbridled and she can demonstrate her love in lots of creative and versatile ways.

Her Vanities
Watch out! All Leo lionesses have huge egos, loud roars and sharp claws (even if she doesn't parade this side to her character too often). Her pride can be insufferable, at times, and she can have a hard time accepting that anyone else has ideas or modes of operating that are as good as her own. She likes to be in the spotlight and she won't hesitate to steal the show, even if it's yours!

Ms Virgo Soul Mate

If you think Ms Virgo is your soul mate, remember that she is an earth sign, which makes her very grounded and realistic. She is one of the most committed signs of the zodiac and she usually means what she says and is devoted to those she loves. But, when love is in the air, don't be discouraged if she initially rejects some of your romantic ideas in favour of more down-to-earth or practical plans.

The Virgo woman adds up to the biggest surprise package of all the zodiac females. So, even if you have known Ms Virgo for many years, when you are dealing with her, the fact that you could have a soul mate connection might just reach out and grab you when you least expect it. When it does, there may be no turning back because Ms Virgo is a lot more resilient and patient than you may have guessed. And she is no easy conquest or open-handed individual either, making her tough to analyse or decipher. Added to this is the fact that Ms Virgo is also very sensitive, psychic, conservative and reserved (something that may not be recognisable at first because of her confident, trendy and friendly behaviour). She isn't likely to be someone who allows you to quickly work her out and, in some cases, you may even need to put on a big act or lead yourself on a merry chase to catch your Virgo gal and make her realise she is your soul mate—or at least that may be what you think! The truth is that she is probably reeling you in much more neatly than either you, or she, realises. Often Ms Virgo is so incredibly coy that it seems like butter wouldn't melt in her mouth. At the same time she can effortlessly wrap you around her little finger with the ease it takes to shake your hand.

Surprisingly for someone with an appearance of being passively natured, Ms Virgo still likes to be the one in control, but she probably wouldn't admit it. She has the ultimate power of control—and that's passive control. You won't even realise she is wielding it, and she probably won't even know she is doing it because it comes so naturally to her. Ms Virgo will initiate 'running the show' or wearing the pants in the relationship in such a clever way you would never recognise just how much she is organising or running your life unless you really took the time to step back and scrutinise who's controlling who.

Once you have a sense that she is 'the one' that fits with your heart, body and soul, to test whether she's your true soul mate, see if she trusts you enough to give up some of her control (even if just for one night). For example, tell her you'd like to take her out on a very special evening, but don't tell her where you are going. Don't allow her to pick the venue, time or place—just tell her what time you'll pick her up and how she should dress. Then observe her reactions and questions. The fewer questions she asks and the less anxiety she has, the better the chances are that she trusts you and is your soul mate. You'll know she is definitely the one when she is prepared to follow you to the end of the earth without question or doubt, because Ms Virgo doesn't like to go anywhere unless she checks her itinerary in advance. She likes to plan out every move—her own and other people's—and if she doesn't have faith in you to make the plans, then you could have a subliminal battle ahead. But if she is connected to you, she'll tune into you and know that what is ahead and what you plan is 'right' without questioning it.

Virgo gals usually hate surprises and dislike anything unexpected because they pride themselves on being prepared. This means that the more willing she is to hand over control to you, the more comfortable she is with you. That doesn't mean you should force your way into the driver's seat more than half the time but, occasionally, if she won't give up the reins, you may discover that she isn't willing to give up or surrender her heart either! And ironically, considering she loves to keep right on top of everything, chances are that one of her secret fantasies is for her soul mate to sweep her off her feet and take command, at least every now and again.

Having said all that, Ms Virgo is well worth fighting for. If you think Ms Virgo is your soul mate, remember that she is an earth sign, which makes her very grounded and realistic. She is one of the most committed signs of the zodiac and she usually means what she says and is devoted to those she loves. Don't be discouraged if she rejects some of your romantic ideas in favour of more down-to-earth or practical plans. Even if she doesn't walk around with stars in her eyes (although there will be plenty of times that she will), when a Virgo gal's soul connects, her heart and soul are yours forever. This soul relationship isn't meant to be immediate or spontaneous; it is one of the most stable and comforting soul mate connections available. Hers is the kind of love that truly can endure any sacrifice—big or small—so be prepared to do the same for her and you both will have a relationship made in heaven.

Her Virtues
Ms Virgo is modest, self-disciplined and conscientious. She'll keep her word, appreciate your gifts and talents, and be willing to help you achieve the things that are important in your life. She has a quiet sort of mystery that will keep you intrigued throughout your soul journey.

Her Vanities
The art of 'worrying' can take on a whole new dimension when a Virgo gal gets going. She can turn herself into a nervous wreck. She can be a perfectionist, which means she's highly critical of herself and others, including you. She can run on high anxiety and might spin her wheels trying to please everyone else instead of doing what's best for her or for your relationship. She sometimes misses the big picture and gets caught up in all the small details.

Ms Libra Soul Mate

Prepare for a bumpy romantic ride. If Ms Libra is your soul mate, she is likely to spin the wheels of your mind and heart all over the place, until you get giddy just trying to work out what this strange interaction between you means.

Being one of the more ethereal, otherworldly gals of the zodiac, there's likely to be some kind of fate or destiny in force when you two cross each other's paths. In fact, it is highly likely that your life is about to become very strange indeed, if you believe Ms Libra is your soul mate. From the beginning you've probably experienced your fair share of confusion and indecision from her about your relationship, so it won't surprise you to find out that more emotional swings, overturned decisions and reversals in behaviour are around the cosmic corner. This soul mate connection can be one of the most rewarding, but also the most maddening, frustrating and confusing, particularly if you're both air signs (that is, born under the signs of Gemini, Libra or Aquarius). But even when you aren't both air signs, Ms Libra is likely to spin the wheels of your mind all over the place until you get giddy trying to work out what this strange interaction between you means.

So before too long has passed, you are likely to be going through all kinds of highs and lows. One day she'll be the perfect gal of your dreams and the next she may be the person who makes you want to tear your hair out. This could turn out to be a very passionate exchange but also one that gets super-frustrating at times. Ms Libra can be a 'material girl' at heart too, after all, her ruling planet in astrology is the indulgent planet of pleasure, Venus. Often she finds it tough to differentiate between marrying a man who can provide her with the best 'lifestyle' or marrying the man who holds the keys to her heart.

To test if she's your soul mate, in a fun way, give her a ring as an expression of your love. It doesn't have to be an expensive ring or an engagement ring, even a plastic ring from a bubble gum machine will work for the test (in fact, it should be a symbolic ring, rather than a real ring). The idea is to see how she reacts to the notion of wearing a ring—even a toy one—from you. Now if she proudly slips it onto her finger or asks you to slip it on for her, there's a good chance you have a soul mate connection, especially if she puts it on her wedding ring finger. But if she says she can't accept it or wears it on one of her other fingers, or because it isn't a real diamond, it should be pretty obvious that the idea of being with you for the rest of her life probably doesn't 'ring true' with her.

Whether or not you try the 'ring test', if you feel that Ms Libra is your true other half, you are in for some incredible lessons in love. As an air sign, she's hard to pin down and she will test your security and trust at every turn. She won't be someone that fits neatly into any description. She'll be clingy, distant, headstrong and easygoing all at once—and you'll never really know exactly what she is truly capable of in the big scheme of things. She's the mystery woman of the zodiac and that only adds to her allure. Her mysterious qualities are just some of the ways she reassures herself that she isn't an open book—and she isn't. If you are in her life to stay, she will make sure that you pass her tests (and she'll have oodles of them for you—tests that exceed anyone's description or expectations).

How do you keep Ms Libra happy, content and feeling secure over the distance that your relationship runs? Well, that can be a tough call. Let her know how much you love her by giving her the freedom she desires, and constantly remind her with words and actions that she is the most important person in your life. As long as you are both honest with each other and keep the lines of communication clear and open, you are certain to have a fulfilling, though sometimes exhausting, soul mate relationship. However, many Librans end up marrying the same person twice, and for them, love certainly seems to be better the second time around.

Her Virtues
Ms Libra is one of the most feminine, alluring gals of the zodiac. She will be affectionate, enchanting and very generous. She believes in fairness and will do her best to be sure the amount of give and take in your soul mate relationship is balanced and equal. Her big heart will keep you warm at night and her deep understanding will assure you that you are never alone.

Her Vanities
Ms Libra can be petty, vain and unbelievably jealous at times. When she's not motivated she can give the word 'lazy' a whole new meaning and she may have a tendency to get depressed and put on extra weight when she isn't being true to herself and her dreams.

Ms Scorpio Soul Mate

Watch out! If Ms Scorpio is your soul mate, you are heading into uncharted emotional, psychological and romantic waters. This is the kind of intense relationship that can sizzle or burn out with such a force that it will leave those it effects feeling as if they need to go into therapy to recover from what they've just been through!

This relationship is the type that will either soar up to cloud nine or cast you down into the depths of despair (or a combination of both) during its rites of passage—even if it is a true soul mate connection. There's nothing simple about the Scorpio gal—everything is intense, extreme and a matter of life or death and her passion, jealousy and intensity burn far brighter and are more challenging than any other gal on this planet. Prepare yourself for a trip to another world of experience if you are aligning yourself with a soul mate born under this powerful sign. Once you two make a strong commitment or connection, your life will certainly never be the same again (on any level of operation).

You are likely to have realised that this is no ordinary exchange of female/male chemistry from your first meeting. This zodiac sign rules sex, passion, desire and a love of power. Whenever a Scorpio is one of the partners involved in a relationship, you are immediately dealing with a personality trait filled with desire that will produce a volatile but extremely enriching exchange. In the air, if the magic truly hits you, you may even subconsciously hear a buzzing of energy flowing between you from the beginning. This is the kind of relationship that can sizzle or burn out with such a force that it will leave those who it effects feeling as if they need to go into therapy to recover from what they've just been through!

Because of the high sexual magnetism and subliminal chemistry given out by any Scorpio soul mate, your connection is likely to be filled with sensuality, sidelong glances and passion from the very start. There's a good chance you wanted to kiss your sexy Scorpio lady (or do much more) the first time your eyes met. Now just because there's chemistry doesn't mean there's anything cosmically connecting you because Ms Scorpio is known for her talent to effortlessly attract men into her life—this is a way she has fun. Even if she's attracted to you, or is just flexing her seductive power muscles, you still need to be aware, because it's just as easy for her to walk away from you as it was to attract you in the first place—but only if she doesn't have a soul mate connection with you. One of the best tests to see if she is your soul mate is to look deeply into her eyes and tell her that you love her. If she's your true mate, your open-hearted declaration of love will make her melt into your arms. If she's not your soul mate, then she'll look away, act anxious and uncomfortable, and possibly even laugh nervously...and then get up and walk straight out of your life!

If she passes this 'I really love you' test, there's an excellent chance that you're soul connected and about to embark on a very special love journey together. When Ms Scorpio realises that she's met her soul mate, she can sometimes let the rest of her life slip through her fingers for a while. Being a person who only knows the principles of all or nothing, love or hate and yes or no, this gal can give her heart so completely, she becomes lost in love. When this occurs she almost sinks the rest of her life like the *Titanic*, and she is so smitten by her feelings, that she makes it impossible to resurrect the world that she had before she met you. Too often she may bring closure to her old existence in a way that she may later regret. Because she can become so overwhelmed by her intense feelings and desires when you enter her heart, she sometimes loses her mind. She may want to run away with you to a private place far away from her job, her friends and her responsibilities, so if you love her and don't want her to burn old bridges, you will have to help her see the value in maintaining the other aspects of her life. But to keep her happy and the fires of passion burning brightly, a weekend getaway once a month or so should do the trick.

If you have determined that Ms Scorpio is your soul mate, you may not see such a powerful reaction from her because not all Scorpio gals are likely to react so immediately to their feelings of a connection to you (but many will). She may have had her heart broken in the past and, if this applies, you may have a challenge ahead of you to prove that you are true. If, instead, she acts cool, disinterested and distant, that doesn't mean that you are not 'the one' for her. Sometimes Ms Scorpio is clever about hiding her feelings and keeping you guessing. Remember that she is a water sign and has the ability to hide some of her deepest feelings. If you are one of the few people she lets into her heart, and you give her a reason to distrust you, it could be a very long time before she will completely open her heart to you again. Fidelity, trust and commitment are very important to her. If you slip up on any of these three components, you may find that you are never forgiven—no matter how much you beg for it. To have the most fulfilling soul journey together you will need to be faithful and extremely honest with each other about your individual needs and values. You'll also need to be willing to make compromises along the way. But if you follow your hearts, and nurture the love you both have, this relationship can take you far beyond your hopes, wishes and dreams.

Her Virtues

Ms Scorpio can be mystical, sensitive, perceptive and relatively independent. She has lots of energy and she'll be interested in sharing work and playtime with you. She's philosophical about life and you'll be able to talk to her about things that you can't with anyone else.

Her Vanities

Ms Scorpio can be obstinate, manipulative and highly critical. When she's in one of her sensitive moods, she can be easily offended and her anger can be explosive. She's not above alienating others, including you, when she can't have her way, and she can pout with the best of them!

Ms Sagittarius Soul Mate

If the Sagittarius gal is your soul mate she is going to be your lover, teacher and best friend. What she brings into your world will throw you right into the thick of exceptional conditions (emotionally, financially, spiritually and psychologically), and you'll soon be dealing with choices that you have never faced before.

Hold onto your hat—if Ms Sagittarius is your true love, you should expect thrills and spills ahead. Ms Sagittarius is the zodiac's free-spirited and most adventurous woman so excitement, challenge and surprise surround her. Her romances, particularly the experience of possibly meeting her soul mate, will be something like the action scene of a dramatic, thrilling, high adventure Hollywood movie—a little of everything rolled into one. A Sagittarius woman is into extremes, abundance and full-on living. She doesn't deal in limitations and her relationships often go the way of extremes as well.

In fact, if you are currently considering a specific Sagittarius woman to be your soul mate, let's hope that you are prepared to embark on one of the greatest adventures of your life, because that is exactly where this high-spirited gal is certain to take you.

From the first meeting (or soon after) you'll find that your head and heart are likely to be spinning all over the place and nothing seems to be normal in your world anymore. Your boundaries are likely to be enormously altered too, because the Sagittarius gal is going to be your lover, teacher and best friend. What she brings into your world will throw you right into the thick of exceptional conditions (emotionally, financially, spiritually and psychologically), and you'll be soon dealing with choices or options that you have never faced before.

Why is meeting your Sagittarius gal soul mate such a challenging and life-altering experience? She's exceptional because Jupiter, the most magnanimous and privileged planet of the zodiac, rules her. Her life is not meant to be mundane or commonplace. That is why a soul mate connection with a Sagittarius gal often begins with high drama, confrontation or a run-in of some sort (or if it doesn't begin that way, it is likely to head in these directions soon after). Ms Sagittarius often appears into your life with a 'bang' as she isn't someone who hides her light under a bushel. She may run into the back of your car (or you'll bump into hers), you'll meet at a sporting event (possibly a ski lodge), or you'll be caught up in an intrigue when she starts to date your best friend, and then you and her fall in love, causing all kinds of complications. She may be travelling, wining or dining or sailing a yacht, but whatever it is, she will be doing it 'her way' and her desire for independence could make her tough to pin down.

Be warned, a Sagittarius woman has a knack for living her relationships close to the edge—in fact, she thrives on it. She often has more than one relationship going on at the same time. Intimacy often scares her and she doesn't always feel comfortable letting others get too close. Innately, she is born with a great deal of independence. She loves to be surrounded by friends, associates and a variety of unusual 'hangers-on' and doesn't fit too well into exclusive one-on-one arrangements, which is why her deep desire to find her soul mate often confuses her. She wants the close connection, but doesn't feel comfortable with it! She won't admit it, but she is so strong within herself that she often looks down on the male sex, especially those who can't keep up with her. Naturally, she hopes her soul mate is even stronger then she is! But that doesn't mean she doesn't want a sensitive, compassionate and gentle man as well. She often looks for one thing in her man, only to discover it is actually the opposite characteristic that she needs the most.

To test if a Sagittarius gal is your soul mate, you are going to need to make some smart moves. As much as you may need to be strong, independent and full of courage, you will also need to find a way to appeal to her soft and vulnerable side—without losing her respect—and that won't be easy! This is the zodiac girl that can easily walk all over her man if he doesn't watch the power exchanges and keep her respectful of his position in the relationship.

What should you do to test whether a Sagittarius gal is your soul mate? Pursue her, and do it with flamboyance and lots of style. She loves drama, so write her a love poem and have it engraved in stone, or serenade her under her window by moonlight. Be daring, creative and romantic all at the same time. If she's your soul mate, even if you do something over-the-top or even a dash ridiculous to woo her, you will know it immediately by her smile. You will practically be able to hear her walls of defence crashing down around her and she will tell you she loves you. She will applaud your efforts at being romantic and playing the role of the pursuer. If, on the other hand, she treats your special and romantic gestures with embarrassment or annoyance, you can be sure she's not the one you're looking for. Ms Sagittarius doesn't play romantic games and if she doesn't want you, you are likely to learn her disinterest in you before too long has passed. As much as this may be hurtful, at least she doesn't waste your time to boost her ego (like some of the other more conniving signs of the zodiac).

However, if you are her true love, she is likely to reward you with the greatest gift she has to offer—her total devoted love. When a Sagittarius gal makes a soul mate connection, she's found a big and important piece of her life's puzzle. Her entire face will look different. Her eyes will shine more brightly and her smile will flash with charisma and the certainty of being in love. It's possible that she'll let her other responsibilities slide for a while when this happens, but she'll get back on track before too long. In the meantime, enjoy her undivided attention and make sure you let her know how much she means to you and your future. Be sure to compliment her on her many talents, cultivate an interest in her friends, family and hobbies, and be prepared to fit in with her master plan for life wherever possible. Remember, even in love, this gal is one of the more independent women of the zodiac and she needs to be adored from both near and far and allowed the leeway to live her own life and to be her own boss when she needs to be!

If you believe Ms Sagittarius is your soul mate, remember that she's a fire sign and has childlike charm and enthusiasm at times, but she can be incredibly intimidating at other times as well. Try not to take it too personally when she lashes out at you, because she is usually angry with herself when she throws her biggest tantrums. Matching up with a Sagittarius woman is a soul mate connection that is destined to be filled with pleasure and pain and it is up to the two of you to find a happy medium between sharing time and giving and taking in ways that add up to fair play. Creating a disciplined balance of give and take between you both will help you nurture your love and make your soul mate journey together the most fulfilling, adventurous, passionate and educational relationship on the planet.

Her Virtues
Ms Sagittarius has the ability to make each and every day feel like it's a party. She can be generous, optimistic, candid and ambitious. Her curiosity keeps her interests fresh and growing and her enthusiasm will easily rub off on you. She has a great deal of inspiration and she will be committed to creating and maintaining the best soul mate relationship that is possible.

Her Vanities
Ms Sagittarius loves to show-off and does whatever she can to attract attention (and there will be times when she will ignore you when she wants to be positioned centre stage

herself). She can be terribly impatient and intolerant at times, and her sharp tongue can cut ribbons through you when you least expect it. She is sometimes self-centred and arrogant and she won't take well to criticism, especially from you.

Ms Capricorn Soul Mate

Although meeting your Capricorn woman may be one of the quieter and less dramatic of romantic connections, nevertheless, this encounter can still be a powerful liaison because the links between you are strong and the two of you are likely to just flow and fit together like magic.

You are in for a total mind, body and soul experience if you are soul connected to a Capricorn gal. In fact, discovering that you have actually met a Capricorn woman who is your soul mate can be one of the most magical connections of all. Fate often plays a profound role in bringing you both together. If the experience of your first meeting is really powerful (and it often is), you will suddenly feel as if you have come home to your heart! When you meet a Capricorn gal that you have a soul mate connection with, it's a lot like being reunited with a long-lost friend, but one with an extremely passionate sexual appeal as well. You'll share an easy sense of comfort that exceeds logical reasoning and your desire to connect with her in mind, body and spirit will be strong, deep and persistent. Lots of Capricorn gals have strong intuition from childhood, so she may sense this soul bond even before you do, but she can be very cautious about the feelings of her heart, so she may not reveal her emotions or desires to you at first. Ms Capricorn is often not too free and easy about expressing her emotions. She likes to be on safe ground before she leaves herself open to any kind of hurt or criticism. But although many initial soul mate meetings (which involve one of the partners, or even both of the partners, being Capricorns) are exciting or predestined by fate, they aren't always so dazzling, emotionally overwhelming, or eventfully dramatic. The realisation that you may have met your soul mate can creep up on you slowly—especially when the gal is born under the patient and very determined sign of Capricorn. Just because you have a soul mate connection with a Capricorn gal doesn't mean this relationship will start off with a rush of cosmic adrenaline or flashes of intuitive lightning between you. Although meeting up with your Capricorn woman may be one of the quieter, less dramatic connections, it can still be a powerful one, because the links between you are strong and well connected.

To test if Ms Capricorn is truly your soul mate, casually tell her a story about an amazing, very attractive, elegant woman you met at work or through a friend, and make sure you mention how interesting and funny this acquaintance was. Leave the story incomplete in some way and see how Ms Capricorn reacts. If she is interested in you, she is likely to become a little put out, or a trifle peeved, but you'll have to watch closely to gauge her response because she can be a great gal at hiding her true feelings. If you sense that she is concerned and may feel that you have an interest in the 'other woman' that's when you tell her that this acquaintance is 75 years old, so that the intensity of the moment can dissipate. Competition is good for the Capricorn gal (otherwise she will play very hard to get). So just leave a false trail or provide a hint that this other woman may be a little interested in you—that way you can bring about a show of emotions from your Capricorn gal, even if it is subtle in form. A really forceful Ms Capricorn is too practical and too possessive to let you get away with another woman without a fight, and if you have a soul mate connection with her, she will often openly compete to hold your attention and interest. On the other hand, if she seems unmoved by your description of the other woman and isn't even curious enough to ask anything further about the matter, then she's probably just enjoying your friendship and doesn't have a bond with you.

If you think you have met your soul mate and she is a Capricorn, you're in for quite an emotional ride, and a strange one at that. She's an earth sign so, in many ways, she's extremely logical and practical, but she can also be very emotional and her actions and reactions can be hard to predict with any degree of accuracy. This soul mate connection will sometimes stretch your limits and patience, but it will be easy to see that she is the only one you truly want to share your life and love with. And there's no doubt that a Capricorn soul mate will dare you to reach for your highest dreams and discover more of your own magnificence. She'll be the finest partner, teacher, lover and companion—and she'll get even better with age!

Her Virtues
Ms Capricorn is open-hearted, reliable and supportive, and she'll be classy, clever and true to herself and her own values. She will be your biggest fan and your most loyal confidant and all your deepest and darkest secrets will be safe with her. She'll be committed to you and your relationship and she will do everything in her power to make sure you both succeed.

Her Vanities
Ms Capricorn can be moody, sarcastic and self-righteous. She is so driven by her desire to make it to the top that she often forgets to smell the flowers along the way. She can be distant and unapproachable at times, and she has a very hard time relaxing. She can also be extremely self-critical and sometimes very 'down' on others too!

Ms Aquarius Soul Mate

A relationship with an Aquarian usually does not follow the normal patterns or timeframes. If the Aquarius gal is your soul mate, you may even get to know her years in advance before the two of you actually make a romantic connection. You may even meet each other, date or flirt and then marry only to separate and then, like magic, suddenly match up again in the future.

Uh oh! An Aquarius gal is always a tough lady to fathom. If you're wondering if you have soul mate connection with Ms Aquarius, you will have your work cut out for you. Aquarians (of either sex) can be the hardest people to pin down when it comes to determining if there's a soul bond between you. Ms Aquarius can be spontaneous, unpredictable, lovable yet remain aloof, switched off and unobtainable all at the same time. She can say yes and mean no, and then add a maybe in between. She is probably the greatest mystery gal of the zodiac (and she likes having things that way!). Ms Aquarius is never going to be an open book, and some of the best conversations she has are with her inner dialogue, so she isn't likely to open up to you all the time. In fact, she could keep a great deal of her secret dreams, hopes, wishes, fears and insecurities to herself indefinitely, even if you are indeed soul mates.

Your meeting is likely to be peculiar or even rather weird, and it may even be that you meet up several times before you actually discover how truly connected you are. Sometimes the most obvious things escape you when an Aquarius gal is involved, because there's always a distraction or something else happening around you that stops the true connection from being revealed. You may even date, flirt and marry, and then separate and, like magic, suddenly match up again in the future.

Now this gal is known for her independent spirit and you'll need to respect her strong, although sometimes hidden, desire to have plenty of space around her (particularly emotionally). She doesn't like to feel cornered or possessed.

To test if you have a soul mate connection with your Aquarian, give her the opportunity to make a choice between dating each other exclusively or dating other people as well. Aquarius gals relish their freedom, but if she feels a soul bond with you, she'll be willing to give up some of her independence to guarantee you return home to her each night.

It's important to realise, however, that even if she is your soul mate, she's still an air sign and that means she can be very flighty at times. In fact, there will probably be days when you wonder if you really know her at all. Don't take it personally; this is just the Aquarian way of maintaining a certain amount of independence and individuality. In fact, the closer you get, the more she can react by going on a sudden vacation with her friends or spending days on end in quiet thought, seemingly cut off from you. The truth is that, at these times, she's more connected to you than ever, and it probably scares her.

Nobody can feel more alone than an Aquarian but then, nobody likes being alone quite as much as this sign either. Ms Aquarius is often caught between her need to be with you and her need to have time to herself to work at her career and to keep abreast of world affairs. However, her desire for you will never really ever be quenched. When an Aquarius girl's soul connects, a deep yearning is fulfilled within her; a far deeper yearning than many other females of the zodiac ever experience. If you are her soul mate, you are the one person she's been wishing for and waiting for her entire life. This can bring a lot of pressure because, chances are, she's built up a lot of expectations that she hasn't truly come to terms with. For this reason, there are sure to be some battles along this soul journey but, together, you can rise above any obstacles and grow from strength to strength in your soul mate connection so that, eventually, it dazzles both of you in its unique brightness.

Her Virtues
Ms Aquarius can be creative, open-minded, resourceful and a bit eccentric in an intriguing sort of way. She can be lots of fun, generally optimistic and enjoy joining in on whatever your interests might be. Her originality will attract all sorts of new ideas and opportunities into your life and she will make you feel glad to be alive.

Her Vanities
Ms Aquarius can be easily distracted, unrestrained in her emotions, and seem to be in a constant state of change. She is sometimes very outspoken in her opinions at some of the most inappropriate moments, and she occasionally sets herself up as an object of ridicule.

Ms Pisces Soul Mate

Expect a surprise a minute if this gal is your true companion. A soul mate connection with Ms Pisces often starts when you least expect it and continues down a most unsteady and unusual path. Because of the strange nature of this connection, you could meet your Pisces soul mate while trying to hail a taxi, riding in an elevator, or while you're out on a date with someone else! Wherever or whenever it occurs, your meeting and the way your romance unfolds is likely to be quite extraordinary.

Feeling bewitched, bothered or bewildered? Well, if you've met a Pisces woman and you're wondering if she's 'the one' for you, you're soon going to be feeling that way. This is the gal who has the invisible power to sweep you off your feet so that your mind, body and soul leave the land of reality and head into the land of fantasy! She is one of the most romantic gals of the zodiac, but she also goes through extreme emotional highs and lows—emotional swings that sometimes see her (and whoever she's involved with), fly quickly off to cloud nine and then suddenly switch direction and crash and burn. Broken hearts happen frequently to this delicate, sensitive feminine gal. Indeed, it is her extreme femininity that can both help and hinder her. Magic is in the air around every Pisces gal and she knows how to conjure up all kinds of emotions, without even trying. She spends a great deal of her life attempting to overcome her emotional highs and lows, but usually they run her, rather than the other way around.

It's likely that your entire encounter with Ms Pisces is off the wall or out of the ordinary in some form or fashion. A soul mate connection with a Pisces gal often starts when you least expect it. You could meet her while trying to hail a taxi, riding in an elevator, or when you're out on a date with someone else. Gloves, umbrellas, lost items and even pets are often involved in soul mate encounters with a Pisces lady. If you are wondering whether a particular Pisces girl is your soul mate, it's better to find out now, because soul mate or not, women born under this sign are very easy to get attached to, whether or not they're your true soul mate.

Ms Pisces is psychic so she's likely to be very open about her feelings toward you. She may mention soul mates very quickly after your first meeting if the chemistry between you is strong. You may know immediately that she is right for you, but there could be some issues to sort out, like the fact that you are both already married, that she is leaving for foreign shores the next day, or some other drama that you need to deal with to ensure you can be together. Usually entering into a relationship with a Pisces woman has its complications and there are some challenges to overcome.

Once you've realised that you may have met your perfect match, to test if Ms Pisces is your soul mate, send her a bouquet of flowers anonymously and see how she reacts. If she tells you about the flowers or suspects they're from you, she is probably hoping you sent them, and there's a good chance she feels a soul mate connection with you. But if she doesn't mention them, she either doesn't have a soul mate level of trust with you or she's hoping they're from someone else.

If Ms Pisces passes this soul mate test, you are probably at the beginning of a very romantic and fulfilling soul mate journey of love. But don't expect your time together to be smooth sailing. Remember that she's a water sign, so there will be times when she will be melancholy and temperamental and you may doubt her love and commitment. When that happens it will be necessary for you to let her know you need to be reassured, without making her feel defensive for her changing moods and emotions. The more open you are with her and the more vulnerable you are willing to be, the more she will trust you and let you into her private world of romantic dreams.

Her Virtues
Ms Pisces can be compassionate, intuitive and highly sensitive to your moods and the thoughts and feelings of the people around her. She can be graceful in her mannerisms and movements and she is probably talented in some form of art or music. She is very non-judgmental and will welcome all of your friends and family members with open arms.

Her Vanities
Ms Pisces can be scattered, anxiety-ridden and easily hurt at times. Her melancholy moods occasionally slip into depressions that can last longer than you'll want them to, and she can sometimes be distracted when you need her to be very focused.

SOUL MATES IN HOLLYWOOD

Finding your soul mate is tough enough, but imagine trying to do it under the scrutiny of the paparazzi and millions of adoring fans! No one knows more about how difficult it is to make a relationship work than those celebrities who live their private lives in the public eye. Reconnecting with your twin half isn't easy when you're famous, so let's see if these well-known couples have got it right.

Pierce Brosnan and Keely Shaye Smith
(Taurus and Libra)

Pierce was born 16 May 1953 and has Venus in Aries and the Moon in Cancer. Keely was born on 25 September 1964 and has Venus in Leo and the Moon in Taurus. These two have plenty of close astro connections but are they soul mates? Probably not! Venus, the planet of romance, rules both signs, so they have plenty of loving, friendly, compatible energy between them but, on many levels, they are poles apart too. Pierce is an earth sign (Taurus), while Keely is an air sign (Libra). Pierce is a fixed sign and very stubborn and Keely is a cardinal sign and far more likely to try new things and then get bored with them. Right there you see how these two are together, despite their sun signs being at odds. Keely's Moon in Taurus puts her emotionally in tune with Pierce's Venus placement in Aries (which makes him quite self-centred) and with Keely's Venus in Leo, this adds up to 'clash of personality' material.

Pierce and Keely may have very different views on life and this could create some tension in the future, especially when it comes to raising their children and dealing with loyalties as well as financial responsibilities. However, they are connected emotionally and are in it for the long haul, but from their horoscopes it doesn't really appear that they are true soul mates.

Out of a possible ten, this couple's soul mate rating is a four.

Madonna and Guy Ritchie
(Leo and Virgo)

Madonna was born on 16 August 1958 and has Venus in Leo and the Moon in Virgo. Guy was born on 10 September 1968 and has Venus in Libra and the Moon in Aries. Uh oh! This relationship has got some major trouble zones and Madonna and Guy may not make it through the next few years. At least, according to their stars, this couple has lots of things to disagree about, which should keep their relationship volatile. In fact, it seems strange that they 'clicked' at all. Mrs Ritchie is pretty demanding and fiercely independent. She is likely to be the one 'wearing the pants' in this relationship, whereas Guy is possessive and proud and wanting to 'take care' of his partner and prove himself. He could find it tough being Mr Madonna! Madonna is extremely demonstrative and active, while Guy is more conservative, reserved and low-key. But having their baby boy will create a huge bond between them and may help them overcome a lot of their minor disharmony.

Madonna and Guy's Venus match-up is a loving one, but when they aren't in harmony, it is likely to get pretty nasty. Her Moon in Virgo is emotionally in tune with his Virgo sun sign—she doesn't take matters of the heart for granted and neither does he. Guy's Moon in Aries allows him to keep pace with Madonna and enjoy being in the spotlight just as much as his famous wife. But this doesn't mean it is enough to help them work through the big stuff!

Out of a possible ten, this couple's soul mate rating is a five.

Antonio Banderas and Melanie Griffith
(Two Leos!)

Melanie was born on 9 August 1957 and has Venus in Virgo and the Moon in Capricorn. Antonio was born on 10 August 1960 and has Venus in Virgo and the Moon in Pisces. This couple definitely has high potential for being soul mates and, even if they aren't, they are certainly sex mates. This couple has a good combination of fire, passion and lust, but the question is, can they live on this? Well, Antonio and Melanie are about to find out! As Leos, they are both fixed fire signs, meaning they are stubborn and prone to temper tantrums (after all, the lion does like to roar a lot!), but they are also very loyal and ruled by their heart, so even when they do argue, they make up more passionately than any other couple!

Just by looking at the fact that both Melanie and Antonio have Venus in Virgo tells us that they are on the same page astrologically when it comes to love and marriage. Venus in Virgo inspires them to try to be 'perfect' for each other, but trying to be perfect all the time (and do the right thing by one another) can become extremely exhausting after a time. Both of them are family-oriented, and this may help them survive the hard times ahead. Melanie and Antonio place great stock in their children and providing a good home for them, and have few close relationships outside of their marriage because people with Venus in Virgo prefer spending time at home with their partners rather than living it up with their friends.

Melanie and Antonio's moon signs are also compatible. Melanie's Capricorn Moon makes her ambitious with a strong desire for a stable family life. Antonio's Pisces Moon makes him sensitive, creative and impressionable.

Out of a possible ten, this couple's soul mate rating is a seven.

Catherine Zeta-Jones and Michael Douglas (Two Librans!)

Catherine was born on 25 September 1969 and has Venus in Virgo and the Moon in Pisces. Michael was born on 25 September 1944 and has Venus in Libra and the Moon in Sagittarius. Same day couple (but different year), Catherine and Michael have a real soul mate connection (and they knew it from the first moment they met). Now that doesn't mean that they will live happily ever after, but it does mean they have a lot of positive energy going for them.

Venus, the planet of love and relationships, rules Libra, an air sign. When two Librans get together, it is usually very passionate but also intellectually stimulating, with both partners possessing a great appreciation for music, art and books. Librans are very indecisive people, however, and it's important that one of them takes a leadership role or nothing will get done! By looking at their Venus and Moon placements, we'll be able to see exactly who the more decisive partner is.

Catherine, with Venus in Virgo and Moon in Pisces, is definitely more passionate and determined than Michael, who is good at starting projects, but not so good at finishing them with his Venus/Moon placement. Men with Sagittarian Moons are inveterate chasers of the ideal woman and Michael has made it no secret that Catherine is just that.

Out of a possible ten, this couple's soul mate rating is a nine.

John Travolta and Kelly Preston
(Aquarius and Libra)

John was born on 18 February 1954 and has Venus in Pisces and the Moon in Virgo. Kelly was born on 13 October 1962 and has Venus in Scorpio and the Moon in Aries. This is definitely a spiritual union, with John and Kelly clearly soul-mate material. There are connections on many levels that help keep this couple together, with enough differences to ensure things don't get boring or routine.

As a couple, John and Kelly work together through the good times and the bad. There is a real sense of teamwork in this relationship, with each bringing out the best in the other. Social interaction is also a high priority for Mr and Mrs Travolta, and this is one Hollywood couple who love to entertain.

When they're not around other people, John and Kelly are likely to have a great rapport and easy communication between them. Both are air signs (Aquarius and Libra), indicating this couple are on the same intellectual wave-length. When it comes to matters of the heart though, John's Virgo Moon is a lot more practical than Kelly's passionate Aries Moon. Still, this provides a good balance between the two and ensures that any emotional dramas (though few and far between) are dealt with rationally. Overall, this is a passionate, understanding and respectful relationship that seems destined to go the distance.

Out of a possible ten, this couple's soul mate rating is a nine.

Paul Newman and Joanne Woodward
(Aquarius and Pisces)

Paul was born on 26 January 1925 and has Venus in Capricorn and the Moon in Pisces. Joanne was born on 27 February 1930 and has Venus in Pisces and the Moon in Aquarius. Astrologically, this is one of those relationships destined to stand the test of time.

Paul's Aquarian Sun works beautifully with Joanne's Aquarian Moon, while Joanne's Pisces Sun makes a strong emotional connection to Paul's Pisces Moon. It's easy to see why this couple appear to have such a deep respect for one another. The synchronicity between their Sun and Moon signs hints at an understanding only possible on the true soul mate level. With their intellect and emotions nicely balanced, this is a relationship built on mutual trust and admiration. Here is a couple that works, lives, loves and plays together, taking immense pleasure in each other's company.

Paul's Venus in earthy Capricorn suggests a practical approach to matters of the heart, with a focus on stability, loyalty and consistency. Joanne on the other hand, with her Venus in creative, intuitive Pisces, is the more idealistic of the two; something of a dreamer and definitely a romantic. Together, there is a healthy blend of practicality and idealism in this relationship. There is also a strong suggestion that Paul and Joanne share similar ideals, making it easy for them to work towards mutual goals.

Out of a possible ten, this couple's soul mate rating is a nine.

Cameron Diaz and Justin Timberlake
(Virgo and Aquarius)

The sparkling Cameron Diaz was born on 30 August 1972 and, while a practical-minded Virgo, she would not usually seem a great soul match for a free-spirited Aquarian like Justin Timberlake. Cameron's chart shows her cool Virgo nature is sexed up to a super-sizzling level by her sensuality planet, Venus, being squared off to Uranus—the planet of lightning zaps and shock power. This gives her a compelling need for sexual excitement and a love of the unexpected—just the thing when you're hanging around a guy who also craves excitement in more ways than one.

Justin was born on 31 January 1981 and while there's a fairly significant age difference between this star couple, with Cameron's mercurial love of youth (and having the Virgo's knack of staying forever young), this should not be too problematic for them. The main issue that could drive a wedge between their possible soul mate connection is Justin may sincerely be trying to give Cameron lots of free time and space for her huge career drive, but unless he sees her willing to do the same for him, with his Mars in Aquarius, he will ultimately change tack and put up a fight to be the number one star attraction—both at home and at work.

Out of a possible ten, this couple's soul mate rating is a 5.

About the Author

Born from a long line of mystics and astrologers, Athena is well known internationally as one of the world's leading astrologers. Athena's regular zodiac columns have appeared in *Vogue* (USA), *The Australian Women's Weekly* (Australia), *Star Magazine* (USA), and *Elegance* (Holland). She has also written the astrology books *Zodiac* and *Zodiac Lovers*, and in conjunction with her friend Deborah Gray, a magical spell book entitled *How to Turn Your Ex-boyfriend into a Toad* and a guide to glamour called *Glamazon: How to be fabulous, famous and flawless*.

Through her astrological, psychic and mystical columns and features, Athena has helped many to rediscover their own power, by mastering the ancient metaphysical sacred sciences.

Think Yourself Thin

In her ground-breaking book, *Think Yourself Thin*, Athena Starwoman shares with you the secrets to developing the power of your mind and how to tap into your psychic senses in order to turn your life into a happier and more powerful direction. With Athena's help you will discover your innate psychic abilities and how to use them to control your thoughts constructively to build up your confidence and willpower. As a consequence, you will learn how to 'think thin', so that you won't need to eat as much food as you did in the past. And the result? You will lose weight faster than you ever thought possible and keep it off—without fad diets, supplements or strenuous exercise. Instead, you will have a different attitude, taste and desire for food, and for everything else too.

So let Athena help you discover and use the mental magic within you. You'll gain unlimited power to live the life of your dreams and get into perfect physical shape!

Glamazon: how to be fabulous, famous and flawless

Good girls may go to Heaven, but Glamazons go everywhere, and they do it in the best of winning style! They always look fabulous and fashionably hip, know how to stir up the perfect martini, get invited to all the A-list parties and can spot the right man (and the purr-fect new shoes) from 100 paces away!

Wickedly entertaining with priceless insights about the world of glamour and how to get there, *Glamazon: how to be fabulous, famous and flawless* is a humorous and sophisticated guide to how women can discover their inner allure and use it to create a life full of potential, power and...Prada. You'll discover the modern girl's winning lifestyle, the path to glamour, fashion and fame and flourish in a self-made world of opportunity and, of course, fabulousness.